MW00882262

Hey Nana!

Hey Nana!

CONNOR'S STORY OF LOVE

Toni Nunemaker

Kendra
Compassion comes
from strength.
Toni Nunemaker

Cover and interior design by Laurie Sienkowski

ISBN 978-1541094932

For my grandchildren, Connor, Kameron, Riley, Morgan, and Zoe, and to all of my children at Excel Charter Academy:

I love all of you with all of me.

Contents

Introduction

This is a story of love and healing after a tragic loss. It begins with my grandson, Connor, a nine-year-old child, who was stabbed to death by a twelve-year-old boy at a playground near his home in Kentwood, Michigan, on August 4, 2014. There was no argument, no apparent reason for the attack. Connor, his brother, and a friend had just met the boy, who, as it turned out, was deeply troubled and wanted to die himself. This boy thought that if he killed someone, the police would kill him in return.

Connor was pure love. You might expect me to say that because I am his Nana, but I am a teacher and have known many children over the years. Connor was different than most children – he lived in the moment, he was careful to avoid hurting anyone's feelings, he regarded everyone as a friend, and he had no enemies. His joyful greeting to everyone was, "Hi! My name is Connor!" He was one of the kindest, gentlest children I have ever known. And he loved us.

It is because Connor loved so well that I was inspired to write this book. I hope his story will become a catalyst for others to love more deeply, to forgive themselves and others more easily, and to cultivate compassion from within their hearts. Connor was simple, straightforward, and honest in his love for the world. I wonder now whether he may have known that he was destined to go back to God earlier than we wanted him to go, and therefore lived full speed ahead to get the most out of his short life.

Having Connor in my life and letting him go has changed

who I am and what I believe. Rather than merely living with the faith and hope that there is a God, I now know there is a God. I live in love because I have experienced God's many miracles. This book is the story of those miracles.

Toni Nunemaker
December 2016

Foreword

I'm considered a hard-nosed reporter. I've interviewed serial killers and rapists, police chiefs, mayors, and governors. Just like a cop, I've found a way to cope with tragedy, with cop humor. It's my shield, the only way to not go crazy. But sometimes, even the thickest shield can't protect you. That's when the tears come.

The death of nine-year-old Connor broke through that shield. All I could think of was my own five kids. How could something like this happen?

Connor was on a playground with his little brother and a buddy. The playground was just around the corner from their homes. They'd played there so many times before, on the swings, the dark green slide, landing softly in the sand. I could see my own son there.

They were headed that way on August 4, 2014, when they found what they thought was a new friend. Jamarion was twelve years old, but looked more like ten. He lived not far away. He wanted to play. But what the boys couldn't have known was that Jamarion had a knife, a big kitchen knife, which he had hidden in the sand. Jamarion struck suddenly, stabbing Connor again and again.

It was a story that horrified a city, an entire state. What could lead a twelve-year-old boy to kill? For months, the answers came slowly — failures by a desperate boy's abusive parents and failures by the state came to light.

What happened to Connor that day, and what had happened to Jamarion before that, made me angry. It led me to dig into the state Child Protective Services system that failed both boys, a system that allowed Jamarion's parents to repeatedly abuse him. The news stories that followed led to major changes that will better protect children from abusive parents.

But even after all of this, what nobody could have understood was the depth of the pain felt by Connor's family. That story is now being told by Connor's grandmother. She takes us onto the porch where her grandson lay dying, into the emergency room where doctors couldn't save him. But most importantly, she takes us into her heart, into the hearts of Connor's mom and dad, into the broken heart of his little brother.

It's a story about love, and the fight to find forgiveness. Perhaps this story will help toward understanding and, just maybe, healing.

Ken Kolker
WOOD TV Reporter
Grand Rapids, Michigan

Traces of Hope

There are times in our lives when the universe shifts from one moment into something completely different the next. Consumed by that moment, you simply cannot stay the same. You must change to be less of who you are or more of who you are. First comes the numbness – a fog that descends on your whole being, settling upon you as you realize there is no way out until you have the courage to push it away and live with your decision. Mercifully, on that day for me, the numbness came quickly.

BAM! Something hit my front door so hard that my walls shook around me. *Was it a bird? No, it couldn't have been a bird.*

BAM! BAM! *Someone was trying to kick in my door!* I knew it instantly, and my first instinct was to escape before the front door gave way. My head felt huge and swollen from fear, even though only a few seconds had passed since the first kick. I heard my heart beating inside my head. *Would I live?*

I glanced out the front door window to see what monster was trying to invade my home. It was my oldest son, Jared. *He has a key, why is he kicking my door?* BAM, BAM!

"Stop!" I yelled through the vestibule door. "Stop! I'm here Jared, I'm here!" I kept shouting until I opened the door. "I'm here, Jared! I'm okay."

Jared was in a rage, and his energy hit me as soon as I opened the door. I felt small inside that energy – his fury and panic were so great. He began sobbing, and he grabbed me.

"I thought you were dead," he cried. "I've been trying to call you and you didn't answer and I thought you were dead!"

"I'm here." I held him, and I said it again. "I'm here. I'm here." With Jared's next words I felt the first wave of numbness begin to infiltrate my body.

"They stabbed my baby! They *stabbed*...my baby!" Jared's rage melted into complete despair. I sensed his need for his mother and felt a bit stronger. Mothers are supposed to be strong when their child is in trouble. But my knees didn't seem to understand this, because with each breath the numbness crept further in. I slipped to the floor, pulling Jared down with me. The numbness wasn't complete yet – just my lungs and knees were engulfed, but my heart still felt everything.

I tried to crawl to the door that led to the garage because I realized that when I had come home from the hospital the day before, I had left my phone in the car. Somehow, I was sure that if I found my phone and checked it, this moment would recede and change into something else that I could control.

Then I saw the blood. Jared had blood on his clothes and hands. There was a smear of blood on his face. Numbness slammed me, and I knew with certainty that I couldn't change this. I would have to hear, see, feel, and know it in every part of my being. In this moment, my universe shifted.

I took a deep breath and let loose the first of my tears, giving in to my despair. It hurt so much that I was afraid I would die from the pain. *Will I totally lose myself in the suffering? Will my mind, body, and soul disappear into the vastness of the anguish that has swallowed me?* For the first time in my life, I chose the numbness to hold back my terror of this immense suffering, which seemed insurmountable.

"*Who* was stabbed?" I whispered, even though I didn't want to know.

"Connor," he moaned.

No, not Connor! I began to weep. I didn't want this to happen to *any* of my grandchildren, so why was this my first thought?

My brain was trying to control what was happening. During a traumatic event, we move almost exclusively to the non-thinking areas of the brain, into the emotional brain, which can only react during an event. And yet, the thinking part of the brain continues to attempt to engage, throwing out traces of thoughts that are seemingly connected and disconnected from what is happening. Our brain creates fractured and random thoughts that only partially fit the moment. My brain was on full alert.

"Who stabbed him? Where is Connor? Is he okay?" Jumbling thoughts began to spill from me. I couldn't stop, they kept pouring out. "What hospital? When did it happen? Let's go right now!" I couldn't even stop talking long enough for Jared to answer. *Why can't I stop?* Everything was out of control. I was numb and stood frozen as the words gushed out of me. Tears and despair and jumble.

"I'll drive. Jump in the car," I finally said to Jared. There. That was something I could control. The first decision was out. I would drive.

As we backed out of the garage, Jared began to answer my questions. Connor had been stabbed in the back, but Jared didn't know who did it. It was a new boy whom his sons had just met. He wasn't sure whether Connor was badly hurt or just wounded, because there had been so much blood.

"Call Aunt Jan!" I yelled. I felt that I was teetering on the brink of insanity. "Tell her to start her prayer circle for Connor." After he talked with Jan, I blurted out for him to call my teaching partner at Excel Charter Academy. "Call Becky! Tell her to have everyone start praying!" I shouted things randomly as Jared spoke to her.

We didn't call anyone else. We couldn't. We couldn't make any more decisions. I could only drive. That's it. I would just drive. The traffic was thick on the highway because it was early evening and people were leaving work. They were going about their everyday existence while we raced toward an unknown.

I begged Jared for more information. "Where was Connor stabbed? What kind of bleeding? What did he say? How was his breathing?" I continued to ramble. I felt sorry for Jared because his mother had become a jumbling idiot. *Oh no, I just thought of myself in third person. I am no longer sane. I will forgive Jared anything, no matter what he says or does from this moment, because his mother has lost herself and he is a poor boy with no mother.*

I gripped the steering wheel all the way to my elbows in

order to control my shaking. Jared continued to explain. A boy on the playground had stabbed Connor in the back. Somehow, Connor had made it back home from the playground and collapsed on their back porch. There was so much blood that Jared thought it was only one wound, but he wasn't sure. The wound was on the right side of Connor's spine, behind the lung.

Jared struggled to breathe. He gasped for air as he explained that the bleeding was arterial, and the wound kept spraying blood unless he put pressure on it. When an artery is severed, a spray of blood shoots out of the wound with each heartbeat. Usually you would put a tourniquet above the wound to stop the severe bleeding, but you can't use a tourniquet when a lung is punctured.

Jared said that Connor kept saying, "I love you, Daddy," and trying to turn over on his back to put his arm around his daddy to comfort him. He asked for his momma so he could tell her that he loved her, too. By the time the ambulance arrived, the whites of Connor's eyes were bloody and his breathing was reduced to labored panting. Jared was sure that the knife wound had pierced Connor's lung. His pupils had fully dilated, taking over his irises. When Jared told me these details I knew our little boy was in trouble. This was bad.

Jared had tried to call me as the paramedics loaded Connor into the ambulance. When I didn't answer my phone, he was torn between going to the hospital with Connor and coming to check on me. When he couldn't reach me, he panicked and thought that I was dead or in trouble at home. He had made the wrenching decision to go to me instead of staying with his son. Connor's mom, Danielle (Dani), rode in the ambulance with him.

As we arrived at the hospital, we saw the ambulance that had carried Connor, abandoned in the ambulance bay. *That looks like the ambulance I rode in just two days ago.* We rushed to park, and as we ran in I noticed that I was carrying my hospital bag. This was the bag I had taken over the years whenever I took one of my boys to the emergency room. Sprained ankle, broken finger, glass shard in the leg. *When did I pack the bag?* It contained books and games and water bottles for the long wait at the hospital. I always wanted my sons to think of the hospital as a healing place, so I would sit and play games and read books to them as we waited for x-rays and doctors. I never wanted them to know about my worry over their well-being. I didn't remember packing the bag. *Does that mean I'm crazy? Or because I packed a bag, could I still be considered sane?* I was so numb that I didn't understand how I was able to walk forward. I did not have the power to make my legs move. Something took over and pushed me forward into an unknown that I didn't want to experience.

The hospital employees led us to Dani's family, who were waiting in the emergency room area. I heard Dani scream in the distance. *Where was she? What had happened? Did she know something that we didn't?* My brain was still a jumble, and I couldn't control my thoughts. Now that we were all together, the fear was overwhelming. We were a herd of fear, standing in the emergency room. Within a minute or two, a man introduced himself as the hospital's social worker. He asked us to follow him into the waiting room. To this day, I don't have any memory of what he looked like – I was too afraid to see anyone.

Dani had already been taken to the small family waiting room. When we joined her, a nun was holding her, letting her scream and rail. *GOD.* This was my first thought of God – when I saw the nun. I was surprised to realize that I had forgotten about Him until now. We had asked my sister and friend to pray, and while that had to do with God, I hadn't actually thought of Him or my faith until I saw the nun. Why did I neglect to think of God as soon as I heard the first kick on the door? And then it hit me: God had given me the gift of numbness to help me survive. It was a gift, not insanity. I was not insane, and I would not die from the suffering. I had forgotten God, but He hadn't forgotten me when I needed Him most. I felt the numbness abate a bit as I breathed in and felt God. One breath. Two breaths. Three breaths. I began to calm down as I consciously allowed myself to join with God. I began praying my way back to Him. He had always been there. I was the one who had left Him.

Dani kept screaming and crying inconsolably, even though the nun was trying to comfort her. Jared wrapped her in his arms.

"What do we know so far?" I asked.

"Nothing yet," the social worker told us. He left to get an update on Connor.

While we waited for news, Dani was able to calm down and talk. She kept repeating that the ambulance driver didn't know the fastest way to the main street when he was leaving their mobile home park en route to the hospital, and it really upset her because she felt time had been wasted. She seemed to be grasping at anything to put life back into her control.

As Dani shared what she knew up to this point, I went back and forth between tears and getting myself under control, almost as if I was cycling between the two. Think of Connor, cry. Think of God, calm down and breathe. Listen to Dani, cry. Ask for God's help, calm down and breathe.

Dani said that she thought Connor's heart must have stopped in the ambulance on the way to the hospital. She had heard the brutal popping sound of the epinephrine shot into Connor's heart, and a few minutes later she'd heard someone say that Connor's pulse had dropped down to four beats a minute. This was confusing for us – did his heart stop, or was it down to four beats a minute? I chose to believe his heart was still beating. It was a tiny piece of hope.

When the ambulance had arrived at the hospital, Connor was immediately taken back into the surgery area, and Dani had been allowed to stay with him. Very quickly, doctors decided to open Connor's chest to massage his heart. Dani was told she had to leave, and that was the moment we had heard her scream.

During the next hour, we tried to piece together what had happened. A little boy whom no one knew had approached Connor, his seven-year-old brother Kameron, and Connor's best friend from across the street, as they played in their yard. Dani had just come home from work and was starting to prepare dinner. The boys ran inside to ask her if they could go to the playground. The buddy system was an absolute with Jared, Dani, and Connor's friend's parents. Both sets of parents needed to agree; they needed to know where the boys were going and how long they would be gone. After confirming that Connor's friend's mom had agreed and reminding the boys of the buddy system, Dani and Jared said they could play for a few minutes.

Within minutes after the boys had left, Dani and Jared heard someone screaming. Kameron came running inside, shouting that Connor had been stabbed. Their neighbor yelled through the back door that they needed to come outside immediately. Connor was lying on the back porch. Jared had been trained as a first responder, so he immediately started assessing Connor's injuries. He asked Kameron to get him something to hold over the hole in Connor's back to stop the blood. Kameron grabbed Jared's swim trunks that were on the floor and handed them to Jared.

Riley, Connor's five-year-old brother, started racing around the house to find the phone to call 911 – Dani and Jared had just taught him how to dial 911 in the case of emergency. He couldn't find the phone because Jared had it in his back pocket. It didn't matter – several neighbors had already made the call and an ambulance was on its way. Riley immediately switched gears when he heard Jared calling out for something to apply to Connor's wounds to stop the bleeding. He tried to find Band-Aids to give to his dad. Riley was in the game, doing everything his little head could think of to help. Three-year-old Morgan remained in the house where Jared had told him to stay, looking out the window, horrified by what he saw on the back porch. He had never seen so much blood.

I heard from others later that Dani kept screaming for the ambulance to come. She thought it took them thirty minutes to arrive – we later found out it was around five minutes. Time is excruciatingly suspended when you wait for help to come, while you watch your little boy slip away.

Once the medics arrived, they worked quickly to assess Connor's breathing, heart rate, and blood pressure. They inserted an IV line to give him fluids. There wasn't anything else they could do to stabilize him, so they began to load him into the ambulance. Jared and Dani both thought that this was when they heard the medics say that Connor's heart rate was down to four beats a minute. As they loaded the gurney into the ambulance, Connor rolled his head and looked one more time at Dani and said, "Momma." The medics closed the back door of the ambulance. Dani rode in the front seat on the way to the hospital.

When the social worker returned, he told us that the surgeons had indeed opened Connor's chest. While he was talking, I envisioned a doctor holding Connor's heart in his hands and massaging it to keep the blood pumping through his body. At the same time, other doctors and nurses attempted to hook Connor up to a bypass machine, which would allow them to work on his injured lung. This was good news and bad news. The surgeons weren't giving up, but they were holding Connor's heart to keep him alive. What do you do with news like that?

A police officer came to our waiting room and told us that the little boy who had stabbed Connor was about ten years old and had called 911 himself to report that he was ready to die because he had stabbed someone. I felt a shock of white light hit my brain when I heard that. I was incredulous. My first thought was that a little boy who had a monster in his head had found our sweet Connor. *I can't care about the little boy right now. I have to stay focused on Connor.* But I briefly closed my eyes and silently asked God to watch over the little boy.

After almost an hour, the social worker relayed the message that the surgeons were still trying to get Connor on a bypass machine so they could repair his lung. This was not good news at all. When I heard this, I knew the golden hour was waning. Doctors refer to it as the golden hour because they have the best chance of saving someone in the first hour after a life-threatening injury. After that, the odds of surviving decrease considerably. The doctors and the emergency teams would soon have to make the decision whether to stop their work and let Connor go. I looked at my son and cried out, "Oh no! They're going to have to call it!"

Jared's response was, "Don't say that, Mom! I can't hear that now." I couldn't stop crying. But there was still a glimmer of hope. They hadn't stopped working on Connor yet.

Within a few minutes we were told to gather because the surgeon was ready to give us an update. Again, we had a glimmer of hope – an update, not a pronouncement. I was dissecting every word to find the hope. Maybe Connor's heart had started and the doctor was coming to say, "Keep praying, he is in critical condition, but he still lives."

The surgeon came in wearing a clean white coat, but he was drenched in sweat underneath and his hair was plastered down. I looked to see if Connor's blood was on his hands, but they were clean. A tender mercy, his hands were clean. I knew immediately, sensed it really, that he had done everything he could – this doctor was good and kind. He sat in front of Dani and Jared and said, "I am so sorry, he didn't survive." His mercifully quick words shattered our hearts instantly.

Everything became surreal at that moment. I sensed an otherworldly energy sweep in to protect my existence so that I could survive those words. I felt a primal wail begin to rise from deep inside me. I tried to hold it back, but I could not stop it. *"Noooo!"*

My heart shattered. I felt as if my body had exploded into molecules and my being was lifted from it. Yet I felt surrounded by all that was good. *Was this God?* Yes, I was sure. I knew I was in the presence of God. Although I could hear what was going on around me, the sounds were muffled. I was in the hospital waiting room, but I was everywhere else in the universe, too. It was the strangest experience I have ever had.

But I was also surrounded by all that was bad – all the horror and grief and pain in that hospital room where my grandson lay dead. I was split between spiritual existence and reality, at odds with each other. I had been transformed by that experience, and I would never be the same. I know in my soul that this happened so I could do so much more than simply survive. But my God, I hurt more than I have ever hurt before.

Everyone in the room cried deep, heaving sobs. I felt as if I were split into two parts: my heart and soul were with God, but my body had been ripped into pieces. I tried to stop my upheaval, but when I thought I could stop crying, I would think of Connor and begin all over again. It was such a strange feeling, to have so little control of my body and emotions.

The surgeon sat quietly with us for a few minutes, letting us weep. There wasn't anything else he could do. He was obviously upset himself. I know that sitting with us must have been one of the most difficult things he had ever had to do. Doctors are used to saving lives, not giving up and letting little boys go because their bodies are too broken to live. We will forever be grateful, knowing that he and the rest of the emergency team did everything they could to save Connor. He quietly told us that the nurses were preparing Connor so that we could see him if we wanted. As he left, I watched him walk away and thought that he had given us the wrong news. He was supposed to tell us that our sweet boy would be all right. This was Monday night, and we were supposed to be eating dinner and laughing and teasing each other. It was the wrong news. I began weeping all over again. *It was the wrong news.*

Not long after the surgeon left, we were allowed to see Connor. Jared and Dani saw him first, then Dani's family. As I waited my turn I thought, *What an odd thing to wait for. "It's your turn to see him now." That's what happens at the doctor's office. You wait your turn. "Next. Yes, ma'am, it's your turn now."* I felt like screaming. I didn't want to be waiting for this turn. I didn't want to see Jared and Dani come back from seeing their son lying dead, holding each other, weeping. But I had to see Connor. It was the final piece I needed so my brain would know for certain that this was real.

As I walked into the room where Connor was lying, I saw nurses, doctors, and policemen standing in a row off the foot of the bed, paying homage to a fallen boy and his family. They stood reverently, quietly, grief-stricken to be standing in this moment, utterly helpless, but compelled to stand guard to pay their respects. It was the first comfort I received from strangers. Their presence seemed holy and pure. They had protected our little boy and watched over him till the end.

The nurses had covered Connor's body completely with fresh, clean, pristine white sheets. I could only see his cleaned little head and face lying on a bright white pillow. They had even cleaned the blood from his hair, and it lay soft and freshly brushed on top of his head, just like I would have done for him. How kind that act of brushing his hair was. There is no small thing.

I wasn't allowed to touch Connor, or hold him, or cuddle him one last time. This was a murder investigation. I had to stand several feet away, and chairs barricaded the perimeter of the bed. I couldn't stand having anything between us, so I moved the chair that was in front of me, clearing a path to Connor.

Where was my hope now? I had spent the past hour and a half steeped in hope, seeing everything through the eyes of hope. In every word I heard, I listened for hope. Every thought clung to hope. I'd had to shift very quickly from a mere twenty minutes before, when I had hoped that the surgeons would keep Connor's heart beating, to the knowledge that God was holding me so I could release my hope and live with something new. I had shifted from hope to love.

I could only stand there, looking at Connor's beautiful face, talking to him. As I wept, I repeated the litany, "My baby, our baby, I love you so." I can't remember how many times I repeated it. A dozen times, maybe more. His little face was suntanned, his nose lightly freckled from the summer sun. *He was alive.* But the intubation tube hung limply from his little open mouth. *He was not alive.* I went back and forth between the two. He was alive. He was not alive. I felt an obsession to know the truth. *Was he alive, or was he dead?* I couldn't wrap my head around the truth – he was dead.

At some point I began talking to Connor as if he were able to listen to me. I had read stories about people's spirits hovering over their bodies after they die. Maybe this was true, and I could talk to Connor one more time. I begged out loud, "Connor, please ask God to watch over the little boy who did this to you. Watch over his family, as they need God's love right now, too. Please surround them with yours and God's grace to help them." I heard a stifled sob from the line of policemen and hospital staff behind me. Somehow it helped, knowing that a stranger grieved, too. I didn't realize it, but the nun had stepped into the room and was behind me. She came forward, gave me a hug, and told me that surely God was listening now and would be merciful. She stepped away to allow me to continue my grieving.

And then the miracle happened. I heard Connor's voice pop into my head.

"Hey Nana! We got this! God and I will watch over you all. I can't come back because I was too hurt, so I'll stay with God."

I stopped breathing. I felt myself suspended in time. I didn't breathe, I didn't blink, I didn't move. Did I really just *hear* Connor?

"It's me, Nana," he replied.

It was Connor! Without a doubt, it was him. I knew the answer, the truth. He was alive.

Everlasting life. I believe it. This was the proof of my belief. Connor was alive. Transformed. With God. What I had, up to that point, only believed out of faith was now an absolute truth to me. God, no matter what you call Him, no matter what faith you live here on earth, is alive. There is no such thing as death – only life, transformed. Connor will always be alive.

Absolution

Many times we assume that it is simply human nature to hold on to hurts, slights, and pain. But, can one choose to say, "No more, I won't carry this one more moment?" Is the extent of our suffering within our own control?

I stood, stunned. Connor was talking to me. He was alive, but his body wasn't. This was overwhelmingly at odds with what was in my head, but not in my heart. In my heart, God was totally present and showing Himself. I was experiencing a miracle that had not been shared with anyone around me. I asked the police and hospital staff if I could stay with Connor longer. One policeman nodded ever so slightly. They were willing to let me stay as long as I wanted.

Relieved, I took a deep breath and went back to the miracle. How long could I stay with God and Connor? Once I left the room, the miracle would be over. Was he hovering over his broken body, just like the stories I had heard? Would he leave to go with God? Would he come back? My heart was broken, and yet God gently held me while I grappled with this tragedy. Questions and thoughts kept running through my head. *Stop*. I needed to clear my mind, release all the questions, and simply be with Connor and God in my heart.

Be still and know that I am God. So I stood. Still.

I don't know how long I remained like this, one with Connor and one with God. My mind had become completely quiet – not a thought, not a flicker. It was like stepping onto a cloud and being fully supported. I felt as if I were deep in meditation. I was unaware of my body, and yet I had an overwhelming feeling of being surrounded by love. This is the closest description I can give of how I felt that day. I was standing in love.

It was Connor who finally made the move to leave. I couldn't bear to be the one to leave him. It reminded me of talking with a loved one on the phone and not wanting to hang up, so you wait till they hang up first. It was easier that way. Connor was always eager to go on to the next thing, so I smiled when he said he had to go with God because he had work to do. But his next words comforted me. He said that he had asked God if he could come back to see me, and God answered, "Yes."

As Connor left, I heard other things in the room again – the humming of a generator, the fluorescent lights overhead, people shifting and breathing. I came back into myself, sensing that I was connected to earth with my body but forever connected to God with my soul. The English language is so inadequate when I try to find words for my experience.

So I live now between two worlds: life and eternal life. My humanity keeps me here with everyday things, but ordinary life is much more magnificent than I had ever experienced, because the other half of me remains rooted in my soulfulness. I sense that I am in both the ethereal and the present all the time. I feel that I am in a constant meditation or prayer state as I live within myself.

This is the gift the universe has given me. It is the answer to my prayers. Ever since I was little, when people asked what I wanted to do when I grew up, my answer was, "I want to know and feel what the old folks feel as they sit on the porch in their rockers and smile." I have won the prize early, at least early enough in my life to live completely differently in the universe. I don't own a rocker yet, but I smile the same gentle, wizened smile that I have seen on old folks' faces as I live between the two worlds. I know what love is.

As I became aware of my surroundings in the hospital room, I knew it was time for me to go. I walked by the men and women who were lined up and softly thanked each one. One by one, they closed their eyes and nodded in response. I returned to the waiting room and sat by myself. When the nun joined me I asked her, "Sister, what happens now? Do we just go home? It isn't possible that we just go home."

I was almost in a panic, begging for things to be different. I couldn't bring myself to leave the room. I felt I needed to sit vigil, to see if there could be a different outcome. Once I stepped outside the waiting room, the tragedy would be real. Our lives would go on without Connor. *No, this didn't make sense. When you take children to the hospital for help, you are supposed to go home with them healed.*

Sister nodded her head and said, "Yes. You must go on."

As I forced myself to walk out, I found the principal of

Excel and all three of our deans waiting for me. We all stood, embracing each other, weeping. Here we were, on summer break, and they had come to honor God's call to be there for me. My heart was completely broken, and I had no choice but to allow them to hold me so I would not sink into the depths of despair and drown.

Over the years, I have told others that I would hold them in my heart and prayers as they moved through hard times, but this was the first time I had experienced it myself. What began with doctors, nurses, policemen, the nun, and my principal and deans continued with hundreds and thousands of people who held my family and me in their hearts and prayers. This demonstration of pure love has been another miracle in my life, and I will always thank God for this special gift of living in love. I have felt cradled in God's love every day since.

After a few minutes with my friends and colleagues, Jared, Dani, and I knew that we had to tell Connor's brothers that he had died. Dani's grandparents had picked them up and taken them to their home while we were on our way to the hospital. As we drove to their home in silence, I found myself counting. At first, I counted my breaths since the miracle, then the minutes since Connor had died, then the hours. Later, I would count the first time I ate without Connor, and so on. For the first month, I counted everything. It was something I had always done when someone died, almost as a commemoration of their life. I count all the firsts without them. It was lonely, counting my losses like this.

When we arrived, we each took one of the boys and sat on the floor. Jared held Kameron, I think because we knew that

Kamcron would need the most support. He could grasp the concept of death, and he had been at the park when his brother was stabbed. He had brought Connor home. Dani held Riley, and I cuddled with Morgan. Jared, Dani, and I looked at each other. I rocked Morgan as he looked at each of our faces, trying to figure out what was happening. I waited, giving Jared or Dani the chance to tell the boys that their darling brother was gone.

Jared finally heaved a sobbing breath and said, "Connor died." Two simple words. Kameron began to wail. It reminded me of my own cry when the surgeon told us that Connor hadn't survived. It was a gut-wrenching sound that brought instant despair to those who heard it. Riley looked around at each of us, trying to figure out what this meant. As it sank in, we all started sobbing, except for Morgan. He was too young to understand.

Morgan asked, "What does that mean?" and Dani tried to explain in between her sobs. I wondered myself, *What does this mean? How can you explain this tragedy to little boys so they understand*? If I couldn't get my head around it, how on earth could they? We sat holding each other, rocking, crying, and trying to answer the boys' questions. We explained what happened in gentle, simple terms that we hoped the boys would understand and be able to process.

Many of Dani's aunts, uncles, and cousins came to the house. We hadn't been able to reach Jared's dad, and my family lived in Indiana, so only Dani's family was there. They spoke in hushed voices. Riley and Morgan, who still did not understand what had happened, began to play with their toy cars. Kameron looked lost, so I asked him if he wanted to go outside for a walk. As we walked around the peaceful yard, holding hands in the cool dark, I told him it was okay to talk about what happened if he needed to. It was okay to cry, be angry – whatever he felt or thought was right. He said he wanted to tell me what happened. I said a silent prayer to God that I would have the strength to hear what he needed to say, and asked God to guide my words and emotional responses

As Kameron spoke, I simply listened. His immediate recounting was limited, although in the next 24 hours he was able to supply more details. I think it was God's way of protecting him as he held back memories. God gently released them a little at a time. I didn't make any suggestions or ask questions while he talked, because if there was a trial, his memory needed to be clear and untarnished. But I could listen.

Kameron said it all began when a boy walked into their yard as he, Connor, and their friend were playing. As we found out later, the boy was twelve-year-old Jamarion Lawhorn. He had walked into the mobile home park from his home, which was several blocks away, with a knife hidden in his hoodie. On the way, Jamarion had stopped and buried the knife in the sand at the playground. Connor, Kameron, and their friend happened to be the first children he encountered. As he approached them in their yard, Jamarion asked the boys if they would be his friends. Connor, true to his nature, said "Sure! My name's Connor. Who are you?" They talked briefly, and then Jamarion asked if they could go across the street to the playground.

The playground was about 150 feet away from Dani and Jared's home. Everyone in the park watched out for all the children, all the time. Dani and Jared could watch the boys in the playground from their back yard. Dani recalled later that she had briefly seen the new boy as he stood at the side of their car, and she assumed he was a boy from the park.

Kameron said that, when they arrived at the playground, Jamarion pulled a knife out of the sand and claimed that he had just found it. The boys gathered around as Jamarion began cleaning it with his hoodie. The three younger boys soon lost interest in the knife and suggested that Jamarion put it back where he found it or give it to an adult. Connor then turned away and tried to show Jamarion the new way they had been going down the slide lately. While Jamarion took off his hoodie, Connor climbed the slide, but he slipped and fell, face down on the ground. Jamarion walked up behind Connor and began stabbing him in the back. Connor never knew it was coming.

Kameron said he watched Jamarion stab Connor, too stunned to move. After being stabbed several times, Connor was able to get away from Jamarion and start running for home, and Kameron ran alongside him. It is the next memory that has stunned us, comforted us, and helped us fall in love with Connor all over again.

As they ran home, Connor said, "Stop, Kameron, and look at me."

Kameron has described what followed next a couple of different ways. He has said that Connor's next words were either "If I die, Kameron," or "I am dying, Kameron." But the rest of Connor's statement has never changed in Kameron's retellings. Connor said, "This isn't your fault, Kam. That boy did this. I will always love you."

Kameron replied, "I'm taking you home."

And so, in one gentle statement, Connor absolved Kameron. By doing so, Connor saved his brother's life, even as his own was ending. And we wonder, how did Connor know that these words would be a powerful gift for his brother? Connor was only nine years old. How could he have known that Kameron could blame himself for the rest of his life for not saving his brother?

How did this wisdom and genuine love come from Connor as he was dying? I have never known anyone who was this calm and wise in a moment of tragedy. Most often, chaos ensues in a crisis, and everyone is screaming and crying and afraid, but not so here. Love was present and calm and gentle. How could a nine-year-old know the perfect thing that needed to be said? God inspired him, without a doubt. I sensed that Connor had immediately been lifted by God and held in His arms, and God's breath whispered the words for Connor to give to his brother. It was another miracle in a night of miracles.

Connor's words protected Kameron's heart and soul and made it possible for him to avoid being stuck in anger, hate, fear, and guilt. Kameron believes that he did everything he could, and he knows that his brother didn't blame him. He knows his brother will love him forever – what a powerful message to receive.

When Kameron testified at the trial, he did not recall

Connor's words as the boys struggled home that day. He said that Connor was talking, but he couldn't remember what he was saying. Jared, Dani, and I have all experienced these scattered memories surrounding this event, so I understand completely why Kameron didn't remember.

For each of us, every memory of that day was coupled with an intense emotion as our brains stored it. When we recall the memory, that emotion is experienced all over again. Memories don't come back whole and pristine – they come back with holes and altered perceptions. This may be why eyewitnesses to an event have completely different stories. I suspect it must drive the police mad when they are trying to determine what happened at a crime scene. Because of this, I began writing my memories down that first night, in order to remember exactly what happened and what was said. While Kameron has forgotten Connor's words, I had them stored on my computer, waiting to bring them back. I will continue to remind Kam that Connor knew this wasn't his fault, and that Connor wanted Kameron to live with love in his heart.

Dani and Jared took Kameron to a therapist within two or three weeks after Connor died. Kameron had nightmares every night, and he was free to climb into their bed when he needed to. His young brain wasn't able to conceptualize and make sense of this tragedy.

Young children who experience a traumatic event often have difficulty throughout their lives with post-traumatic stress because their mid-brain structure changes. While difficult to overcome, healing is possible with consistent work and effort. Children are not meant to suffer like this. Kameron knows he can talk to us at any time. Fortunately, he does.

That first night, Kameron couldn't bear to see the park or the back porch where Connor had lain bleeding. He could not relive that night, and we didn't have the heart to make him return to his home, so Jared's family came to live with me.

For the first week or so, I encouraged Kam to sit on my lap each day. We held each other and talked about anything he needed to talk about. I was amazed at how willing he was to talk about what happened and how he felt about it. Jared, Dani and I told him not to hold in emotions or cover up any pain or anger. We shared how we felt as we went through a different set of emotions every day, sometimes every moment. We shared constantly about Connor and how much we loved him. Kameron was amazing, and Jared and Dani continued to support him in every possible way.

For the first few weeks after Connor was killed, every black man or boy that Kam saw turned into Jamarion. Kameron was convinced that he saw Jamarion everywhere. This was out of character for him. Connor and Kameron were students at Excel, where I teach; the student body is very diverse, representing over fifty countries, so Kam had friends and classmates of all cultures and backgrounds. Yet in these instances, he couldn't grasp that Jamarion was in jail and would never be able to come after him. In Kam's mind, Jamarion was a monster who might appear at any house or playground. In Kam's brain, Jamarion was tangible, not imagined. At seven years old, there wasn't any way his brain could make sense of this irrational fear. After working with a therapist, Kameron has learned that when he is seized by this fear, he should ask himself the question, "Is it really Jamarion, or am I just afraid that it's him?" He has been given the tools to talk himself out of his fear, which allows him a sense of control in his life.

Even so, it seemed that whenever Kameron saw a boy who he thought resembled Jamarion, we would need to look closely and compare. Are the teeth the same? How about the smile? Compare their hair. How large is the forehead? It was a litany that helped Kameron objectively observe the child instead of confusing him with the frightening memory in his head.

We knew that Kameron would be called to testify in court against Jamarion, and we wanted to prepare him as much as possible for the experience. Kameron had never even seen the inside of a courtroom before, so one day I had him watch a court show on television with me to give him an idea of what he would be facing. We talked about who the judge was and where he would sit, and who the defendants and prosecutors were as we watched a case on the show. I explained that Kameron and his friend were called witnesses, and that they would sit by the judge and promise to tell the truth before the prosecutor and Jamarion's lawyer asked them questions. Kameron said he didn't want to see Jamarion and wanted to know where he would be sitting. I told him that in America, anyone who was being tried for a crime had the right to sit where he could see the witnesses, but that police guards would be there to make sure Jamarion couldn't hurt anyone.

Kameron continued to worry that Jamarion would be able to come after him in the courtroom, so one of the district attorneys, Jared, Dani, and I took him to the courtroom where

Jamarion's trial would take place and showed him where everyone would be seated.

When Kameron still had nightmares about Jamarion pursuing him, we asked one of the district attorneys if Kameron could see Jamarion before the trial, thinking this would help him deal with his fear before he had to testify. She spoke with the judge, and it was arranged for Kameron to come to one of Jamarion's hearings. Because Kameron was a witness, he wasn't allowed to hear any of the court proceedings, but he was allowed to be there when Jamarion was brought into the courtroom.

At the hearing, two police officers walked Jamarion into the courtroom and stood guard over him. As soon as Kam saw Jamarion, he looked at me and said, "He's small! He's just a little boy!" The monster in his head died that day when he saw that Jamarion was really just a young boy himself.

In the year following the incident, Kameron was also petrified of knives, especially kitchen and steak knives like the one Jamarion had used to stab Connor. On one occasion, Dani took Kam out to lunch, and he began shaking and backed away from the table because there was a knife on it. Dani asked the waitress to remove it, which helped Kameron calm down. At home, when we were cooking or using a knife at the table, Kameron would talk about how our knife was the same or different from the one Jamarion used.

When Kameron testified at the trial, unbeknownst to all of us, the lead district attorney showed Kameron the knife that Jamarion had used. We had not told either of the attorneys about Kameron's deep reactive fear of knives, particularly the one Jamarion used to stab Connor, so what was meant to be a straightforward identification process turned out to be a gut-wrenching moment for all of us.

The district attorney placed a box in front of Kameron and asked him if he recognized what was in it. Kameron looked into the box and gasped, "Is that the knife?" The attorney said that it was, and Kameron backed away, turning his head and covering his eyes with the back of his hand as he moaned in fear. There was no doubt that he was terrified at the sight. Everyone in the courtroom gasped at his response, and people wept for him. We could see on the jurors' faces that they were affected by Kameron's instant gut reaction. The district attorney was surprised as well, and he immediately removed the box from the witness stand and put it away.

Before he went up to testify, I had told Kameron to look at me if he was afraid. I told him I would smile and help him feel calm, especially if he was afraid of Jamarion. So when he panicked at seeing the knife, I felt terrible for him. He looked like he was going to run, so I caught his attention and mouthed, "You can do this Kameron, hold on!"

As Kameron held my gaze, I nodded to him and smiled to reassure him as he collected himself. He was a little boy, traumatized all over again by seeing the knife that had killed his brother. We hadn't told him that he would have to identify the knife – that was our mistake, not his.

It has been quite a journey watching Kameron grow and begin to heal throughout this tragedy. He has shown great courage and fortitude throughout as he spoke at Connor's memorial service and testified at the trial. This child didn't deserve any of this pain and suffering in his young life, and he will be forever changed. I know that in my own life, my struggles and challenges have made me who I am today, and I wouldn't change any of the life events that shaped me. Even though healing seems an insurmountable task right now for Kameron, I wonder what life will present to him, and what calling will rise to meet him as he begins his service to humanity and the universe.

Connor gave Kameron the most wonderful gift when he absolved his brother of responsibility for his death. If Kameron, in turn, is able to forgive Jamarion, he will have overcome a hurdle that many adults could not overcome: forgiving the person who murdered his brother. Connor's compassion, love, and understanding of what Kameron needed in that tragic moment could be considered a miracle in Kameron's life. I believe that greatness arises from miracles.

Honoring Life

"Your children are not your children. They are the sons and daughters of life's longing for itself. They come through you but not from you. And though they are with you, yet they belong not to you." – Kahlil Gibran

After we left Dani's grandparents' home the night Connor was killed, I was engulfed by numbness. The pain I felt was so overwhelming that I could do nothing but breathe and feel the intense loss. I couldn't think, talk, eat, or sleep. Slowly I inhaled – one breath, then another. I wanted to stop breathing so the pain would go away, but my body was insistent. Each intake and release of air began to cushion me, another breath further from the moment of Connor's death. Hours went by before I could think again. There were things to be done. Thousands of breaths later, I could talk again. It took three days of breathing before I could eat, and many more before true sleep would come again.

The circumstances of Connor's death removed the need

for us to plan his funeral immediately. We were told at the hospital that the coroner's office would hold his body until an autopsy was performed and the murder investigation was complete, which might take up to a week, maybe more.

The morning after Connor was killed, Jared, Dani, Dani's mother, and I took Kameron to the police station to give his formal statement. He was so brave and determined – I had never noticed these traits in him before. On our way to the interview, Kameron told me that he didn't want to be left alone at the station. He said he could face the police as long as he wasn't alone. I promised him that we would be there.

When we arrived, an officer took Kameron's statement while we talked with the detective who had been assigned to the case. When the officer returned to the room alone, I asked her where Kameron was. She said he was waiting in the office. I grabbed my things and ran out of the room to find him. I forced myself to slow down, take a deep breath, and remove the look of panic from my face as I entered the office where he sat alone, swinging his little legs in a big chair. I didn't want to scare him, so I sat down next to him, gave him a hug, and asked how the interview went.

"Good," he replied. I took another breath.

As we prepared to leave the station, we saw that reporters and cameramen from two local television stations were waiting outside the building to speak with us. We then initiated the first move in our campaign to avoid the press. The detective led Jared and his family out a back door while Dani's mother and I went out the front, pretending to be talking animatedly about something. We ignored the reporters, and they did not recognize us. For the next week, we always had to be aware that the media had a story to tell and that they wanted us to be part of it. It was never our intention to prevent the press from telling the story, but we couldn't talk yet. All we could do was breathe.

Two family friends realized that Jared and Dani's neighbors and friends needed to do something to honor Connor's life, so they planned a vigil at the mobile home park for Wednesday evening, two nights after Connor died. For our family, it was the first stage of memorializing our little boy. While Dani and Jared vacillated about attending, I knew that I wasn't ready to talk. I could not go to the vigil. Our family felt it was important to be represented, so we made a poster on which each of us wrote a memory of Connor. His brothers drew pictures. We weren't able to sleep Tuesday night, so at 3:00 a.m., Dani and I drove to the park and tied the sign to the slide from which Connor had fallen.

Dani's mother and uncle attended the vigil on the family's behalf. Over one hundred people attended the vigil, mostly neighbors and close friends of our family. Dani's uncle spoke at the gathering, imploring the children to take back their park and make it theirs once again. Everyone sang "Jesus Loves Me."

Connor and Kameron were Boy Scouts, and Dani's mom was one of their leaders, so several boys from their troop also attended the vigil. The evening ended with the traditional Boy Scout closing ceremony, which now had a new meaning for the boys as they repeated, "Oh Great Master of all true Scouts, be with us until we meet again." It was their first step towards healing. There were tears and hugs, and children and adults left stuffed animals at the playground in Connor's memory. I can only imagine how difficult it was for the children to take back their park – it took weeks before the boys and girls from the neighborhood returned to play.

Excel was offering a summer school session on the week that Connor died. One of Connor's teachers shared that, when our students heard that Connor had been killed on a playground, they believed it to be Excel's playground. Some students initially refused to go outside for recess until teachers explained that it was a different playground. Connor's death touched so many lives in ways we still don't understand.

The funeral home notified us that Connor's body would be released Thursday morning, and we would be able to see him that evening. This was our next step in letting him go. Connor had once told his parents that he wanted to be cremated so that he could be everywhere when he died. We went to the funeral home with family members and close friends, and his body was scheduled for cremation the following day. Connor had loved the television show *Doctor Who*, so Dani found a potter who made an urn shaped like a TARDIS, Doctor Who's machine that travels through time and space. This would be used to store Connor's ashes.

The viewing allowed us to privately say our goodbyes to Connor. It was a very emotional time, but it was a necessary experience for me because I felt reality setting in as I looked at him. We had not been allowed to touch Connor at the hospital, but at the viewing I lifted the cover to see his little feet, still muddy from running outside barefoot just three days before. I held his hands for the last time and tried to memorize his face, including little things I hadn't noticed about him before. It reminded me of when he was born and how we had looked him all over to check his feet, fingers, mouth, eyes, and ears, making sure he was normal. But now it was the reverse. I looked one last time to see if he still had Grandpa's nose, his dad's mouth, his momma's ears. He seemed so little and so still.

Incredibly, our time with Connor's body that night helped us to begin feeling alive again. Life was moving forward, whether we were ready or not. Until this moment, only Connor's brothers had been eating. We adults could not think about putting food in our mouths. But somehow, after seeing Connor, we were ready to share a meal together.

Jared wanted to go to Red Lobster, so we caravanned to the restaurant, only to find that the manager had just released the wait staff for the evening. One of the waiters happened to walk by, and he volunteered to stay and serve us. It was exactly what we needed. For this first celebration of Connor, we had the restaurant to ourselves. We didn't have to be concerned about offending other diners with our stories about Connor, or with our tears and laughter that followed each story. The waiter was marvelous, serving us with a joyful heart. He could not have known the magnitude of the gift he gave us that night.

The viewing had become our unplanned memorial service for Connor, but we realized that many other people needed to see us and say goodbye to Connor. One of Dani's family members attended Cornerstone Church, which turned out to be a perfect setting for the memorial service.

Our family met with the minister on Friday morning to plan a ceremony for the following Wednesday. He wanted to get to know us and to learn something about Connor, so we shared many stories, sometimes laughing and crying simultaneously. We were able to plan something that would allow people to first spend time visiting with us, then celebrate Connor's life during the memorial service, and finally, break bread together. It seemed as if we were releasing Connor in small pieces, so that we could bear the pain of living on without him. It would have been too much to feel at one time.

I planned a private service for myself exactly one week after Connor was killed. At 5:30 the following Monday evening, I visited the playground at the mobile home park to spend some time where Connor had last played. I had heard that the neighborhood children hadn't returned yet, so I thought I could be alone, but reporters and cameramen were there, filming a segment for the evening news to notify the public about the upcoming memorial service. I decided to stay in my car because I did not want to be noticed, but the park manager saw me from her office window and came out to talk with me. When I told her why I was there, she asked the press to step back and allow me to spend some moments on the playground by myself. I was touched by her gesture, and the press respected her request. They stopped filming as I stood holding on to the slide that Connor had climbed only days before.

When I returned to my car, I prayed and cried; I sang along to a CD of one of Connor's favorite songs that I used to sing with him. I was trying hard to believe that all of this was real. These things happened to other people – how was it possible that it happened to us? One week later, and I still couldn't wrap my head around our tragedy.

The day before the public memorial service I took the boys for haircuts. The greeter asked our names and pulled up their records on the computer. She asked who would be getting cuts today: Connor, Kameron, Riley, and Morgan? I stopped breathing and stared at her. What could I say to make this easier?

"Just Kameron, Riley, and Morgan today," I whispered, hoping my grandsons hadn't heard.

I looked down at the boys beside me and saw their blank faces staring back at me. They had heard, and they weren't prepared to handle this any better than I was. Finally, Morgan looked at the greeter and, using Jared's words from the night of the tragedy, said simply, "Connor died."

Connor's favorite hair stylist was sweeping up from her last cut, and she stopped mid-swing when she heard Morgan. She looked at me and said, "I knew it was my Connor. I was sure when I saw the news that it was my Connor who had died."

It was so endearing that she felt Connor belonged to her because she had cut his hair so many times. She had loved the fact that, every time he went in for a cut, he wanted a new style. They would pore over the books of pictures, trying to decide the next unique look. He loved the creative opportunity to become different each time. We hugged and cried, and she told us that it was her last day at this salon. She was so relieved that she had been able to say goodbye to us and share her grief and sorrow over Connor's loss. As we were talking, I glanced at the greeter. She was hitting the backspace on the keyboard.

"*Noooo!*" I screamed in my head.

She was deleting Connor from the computer. I couldn't even breathe as I watched her hit the backspace six times, one for each letter in Connor's name. I wanted to yell, scream, and beg her to stop. *Don't take Connor away!*

The woman looked up and realized that I had stopped talking and that my eyes were glued to her hand. She immediately apologized and said she would finish later. But the wound had already been reopened. I forced myself to breathe. This was how life was to be from now on – moment by moment, erasing evidence of Connor's presence so the rest of the world could go on without him. This was our heartbreaking reality.

The day of the memorial service is blurred for me, and I have asked friends and family to help me fill in the gaps of my memory. I think I was on the verge of a complete shutdown as I attempted to block my excruciating emotional distress.

Dani and Connor's godmother had stayed up all night putting together trifold displays of different aspects of Connor's life – family pictures, baby pictures, school, scouts, dancing, and sports. I was amazed at all the ways in which we would be able to remember him. He had wanted to try everything that life had to offer. Connor's favorite things were gathered, to be displayed at the memorial service: his skateboard, soccer ball, and the last book he was reading, *Diary of a Wimpy Kid*. The pictures and memorabilia were the perfect reflection of his life, and we were touched by the displays.

My youngest son, Keevan, and his girlfriend had flown in from California. She woke up early that morning and prepared a wonderful healthy breakfast for us, but I struggled to eat once again. On this day, I was emotionally right back to where I had been ten days earlier when the surgeon pronounced that Connor had not survived. I was struggling to simply keep breathing.

While several of us had planned to speak during the service, we were all surprised when Kameron declared that he would speak as well. He wouldn't tell me what he was going to say, even though I asked if he wanted to practice. I wanted to make sure he was prepared, so we arrived at the church early to walk him through the memorial service.

When Kameron and I entered the sanctuary, the sound crew was playing the CD that Dani had made of some of Connor's favorite songs. Television and newspaper reporters were setting up in the back to record the service. Because so many people in Grand Rapids had been supportive, and because none of us had yet spoken with reporters since Connor died, Dani and Jared had agreed for the press to make a sound recording of the service.

Kameron and I walked onto the stage so I could show him where he would sit before and after he spoke. To help him feel comfortable with the microphone we sang "Child of Mine," a favorite of Connor's that was playing through the sound system. Because he was so short, Kameron would have to speak in front of the podium rather than behind it, so I had him walk around with the microphone to practice. I reminded him that he could change his mind if he felt uncomfortable with the idea of speaking in front of all those people, but he assured me that he had something to say. Once more, I marveled at his strength of character.

The visitation before the service lasted an hour, and even though we spoke with as many friends and relatives as possible, we didn't get to everyone. Hundreds of people had come to mourn with us. Becky, my teaching partner, played a piano prelude of some of Connor's favorite songs by Bach, Beethoven, and the Beatles as people moved into the sanctuary for the memorial service. When we were all seated, Boy Scouts in their blue shirts, blue jeans, and tennis shoes carried in lowered flags out of respect for Connor and posted the colors. We all joined to say the Pledge of Allegiance.

After the opening prayer, Bruce (Connor's first grade teacher), Jared, and I walked on stage to speak. While Bruce shared how kind, caring, and loving Connor had been, I had a moment of panic. I had not prepared anything to say. Instead, I had prayed the night before that God would inspire me to deliver His message. My confidence that God would give me the perfect message the night before now turned to fear. As Bruce finished, I stood up, took a breath, and gave the following message:

> *I was born to be a Nana. Of all my roles in life, this has been my greatest and most inspiring one – Nana.*
>
> *Our first thoughts a week ago were questions of "Why?" "How could this happen?" "This is a senseless tragedy." And when you ask the universe big questions, you get big answers. The answer we got was: This*

makes perfect sense. We don't like it, but it makes perfect sense.

You are the wonderful village who cared for Connor. When he cried, laughed, slept, ate, played, hurt, and needed comfort, you were all there for nine years. And the truth is, because you were there constantly, Connor's life was magnificent. That makes perfect sense.

But the other side of the truth is that we have thousands, hundreds of thousands, and even millions of children in our world who do not have this village. Their village may be only one or two in number, not a whole village to care constantly for the child and give him what he needs. They are not a fitting village to support their child; they are not enough. The human spirit wasn't designed to grow without others around them. And so the children are lonely, hungry, and in great pain themselves. This, too, makes perfect sense. And that is the tragedy.

So what is the answer?

We could not get Connor to work in his Bridge Book this summer, and I'm a teacher! He has completed a summer Bridge Book since he was in kindergarten. But he kept saying, "I don't need it this summer." Maybe he knew something we didn't. He even hid his workbook so he wouldn't have to do it. But instead, Connor chose to learn about the teachings of His Holiness, the 14th Dalai Lama. I've never known a nine-year-old who wanted to read about the Dalai

Lama for his summer study.

Here's the teaching that captivated Connor: he was amazed that, foretold at birth, a little boy became His Holiness, the Dalai Lama, and was raised to teach his people how to live a life of love. The Dalai Lama teaches that we should make every breath, every movement, every spoken word, and every thought one of complete love. We should constantly be conscious of "being" love. Then, the trick is to see that everyone and everything outside of our self is a reflection of our love. We should recognize love in everyone and practice a purer perception of others, only seeing their great qualities. Connor loved that concept.

"What if we all lived this way all the time?" he asked. "And Nana, can you imagine what the world would be like if every child was raised this way, if every child was raised to be honored and experienced only love from the moment they were born?"

Connor was working on "being" love. What if everyone in our village lived this way?

Hold that thought.

Over the past week, we have heard and received the phrase, "Our hearts and prayers are with you."

That intention from hundreds of people has transformed my life. Scientists can actually measure our heart energy – a normal adult's heart energy is as large as a football field. Imagine all those football fields of heart energy. And that heart energy is the strongest energy in the universe – love.

Our hearts shattered in an instant, and all of you rushed in and held our hearts in yours. It was an absolute, incredible experience of love. I have said and meant the phrase, "My heart and prayers are with you," but until now I have not had the experience of being loved by thousands of people. I am not the same because of it. And I ask you to keep holding our broken hearts for a while longer as God heals and mends them.

So what if all three of these ideas are the answer: the concept of a village raising each child; the Dalai Lama's teaching of love; and your total loving heart energy used to hold each other up? Maybe you were like us last week. After Connor was killed we said, "Close the village gates, bring the children inside, bring out the weapons to protect our children and ourselves."

But maybe the answer is to open the village gates. Bring every child, parent, and family member inside the village and surround them with our love. And when they experience us holding them in our hearts, they will be transformed by love's energy.

We have much work to do. Let us not stop until every child is inside Connor's village. It makes perfect sense.

To each of you in our village, I thank you from the bottom of my broken heart to the top of my soul. The God in me sees the holy, magnificent, joyful God in you.

Namaste.

I was content that I had shared the perfect message from my heart. It was important that, despite my pain, I would speak of love.

Our next memorable message was from Jared. He remembered a time when he was preparing dinner, and Connor had asked the question, "Dad, why are we here?"

Jared replied, "We are fixing dinner, Son."

"No," Connor pushed, "I mean why are we here? What's the purpose of it all?"

Jared answered, "We are here to be good men, to love unconditionally, and to be of service to others."

Jared said that Connor had accomplished these tasks better in his nine years than he himself had in thirty years.

Dani, her best friend, Connor's godmother, and Kameron walked on stage next. When it was Kameron's turn, the whole audience was hushed, and people seemed to be holding their breaths. I said a prayer for this little boy in his Cub Scout shirt. *Please help him find the strength to speak in front of hundreds of people about his brother.*

Kameron didn't hesitate. He began to speak about how Connor was in a better place, and that he was sure that Connor wouldn't want us to be sad all our lives because he had died. He spoke confidently about how Connor would want us to be happy, even though it would be difficult. I could sense the audience members begin to breathe as he shared his seven-year-old words of wisdom. Dani gave him a high five when he finished. Afterwards, many people shared how much Kameron's courage and words had meant to them.

Dani read a poem titled *Do Not Weep for Me* by Mary

Elizabeth Frye. Her friend shared how well Connor loved others and how much she would miss him. Finally, Connor's godmother spoke poignantly of her experience as his godmother and how he had touched her life so positively. She spoke of how much she loved hearing stories about Connor in the past week, and of our strength as a family, which gave her confidence that we would prevail in the coming weeks.

Next, the minister asked the audience to shout out words that best described Connor. Love! Smiley! Amazing! Nice! Caring! Happy! Funny! Polite! The words flew from the audience and landed as gifts upon my ears and my soul. Connor had been so cherished by these people who surrounded us. The minister ended the service by sharing some of our stories about Connor, and we closed in prayer. The Cub Scouts lined the aisle in a final salute to Connor and his family as we left the sanctuary.

The Boy Scouts and their leaders served the meal afterwards. The boys were so impressive as they served and cleaned up afterwards, demonstrating a heart of service as they worked, remembering their friend and fellow scout. Friends said that the Boy Scouts' participation in the memorial service provided the dignity of a military funeral; watching little boys honoring their fallen friend had captured their hearts.

The memorial was instrumental in easing my sorrow because it had been a shared experience with so many loved ones. As I left, I walked around the parking lot to each of the press vans and thanked them for their discreet and respectful handling of our time together. Throughout the whole event, I didn't feel that the press had intruded at all. My impression of news reporters changed that day.

With the end of the service, it was time for us to begin living on without Connor. It was a new beginning in an odd sort of way. Friends and family who had flown in to be with us flew home again, but we knew they were holding our hearts to shore us from what lay ahead.

Always One

My heart broke ahead of time. I am so thankful for that.

Connor was stabbed on Monday evening around 5:30 p.m., but three days earlier, about 5:30 p.m. on Friday evening, my whole being knew something was about to happen. Normally, my life is remarkably stress-free. As a music teacher, I sing and play with children all the time. But on this Friday evening, like a thunderstorm that engulfs the sky with darkness, my whole energy changed from the inside out – it was something totally foreign. I had never experienced this before. I paid attention, and was given another miracle.

At first, the thought crossed my mind that I was having a panic attack. I had heard about them, but had never experienced one myself. What on earth would I be panicked about? It was Friday evening, and my whole weekend was free. I had no obligations for the week ahead, and was looking forward to it.

My jaw began tightening up. *Had I dislocated my jaw*

again? One side of my jaw has been dislocated so many times that often, if I bump my chin, the jaw slips out of place and swells up. I couldn't remember if I had hit my chin on anything, and this did not feel like the same type of pain. My jaw now felt like it was clamped in a vise. My left shoulder began to ache deeply.

I went to the kitchen to take an ibuprofen and drink some water, and spotted the bottle of baby aspirin next to the ibuprofen. I never take it, but I have it on hand because the EMT who taught the Red Cross First Aid Course I had taken three months before had said that, if you are over fifty, you should have baby aspirin everywhere, just in case you have a heart attack. He said to immediately take two aspirin as soon as you have symptoms. *Okay. Notice the little things.* I saw the aspirin, but I didn't really know what was happening in my body. *Would it hurt to take two?* Now I began second guessing myself. *Had the trainer said to take baby aspirin if you are having heart attack symptoms, but not if you are having stroke symptoms? Or was it the other way around?*

Returning to the living room, I let the ibuprofen take effect and Googled it on my phone. "When should you take baby aspirin, heart attack or stroke?" *Ah...heart attack. Wait. When did I make the leap from what's happening – jaw dislocated, panic attack – to heart attack? Am I having a heart attack?* I walked quickly back to the kitchen and swallowed two baby aspirin. *Let's thin that blood out, just in case.*

I then remembered something significant that had happened during the Red Cross course. When we were learning about heart attacks and strokes, the trainer had stopped teaching suddenly and said, "I'm going to talk to someone in here. One of you – and I don't know who, but you're a woman – is going to have a heart attack soon. I just feel it, and I feel compelled to tell you ladies that your symptoms are very different from what men experience when they have a heart attack."

At that very instant, I knew he was talking to me, even though I had never had any of the symptoms he was describing. The trainer continued to describe women's symptoms compared to men's, stressing that if you pay attention to those early symptoms, doctors can stop the attack and save your heart from damage. He said that most of the time, people have mild symptoms, sometimes even weeks before the actual heart attack, and if you go to the hospital rather than ignore the signs, you can avoid a full-blown heart attack.

Wait another minute. What happened last Monday night? My left arm had started aching, and I thought I had dislocated my jaw. I'd had these symptoms the previous Monday night, but not as pronounced. That night, I had taken a couple of ibuprofen, and the symptoms went away. I rarely take medications like ibuprofen, so the fact that I had taken it twice in one week was significant to me now. *Add up the evidence, Toni.*

Heart attack. Is it possible? No, I don't want to overreact. Calm down. Watch some TV. Let the medicine work. Wait half an hour and decide. While I tried to watch the news, I did more research on women's symptoms in the case of a heart attack. Jaw pain and left shoulder ache were on the list.

Make a decision. The pain is still strong, as was my premonition that something big was going to happen. *Call an ambulance? No!* I didn't want sirens and emergency technicians everywhere. *I have to call Jared. Yes, that's what I'll do. I'll call him like nothing's wrong and then ask his advice.* Jared worked third shift, and I wasn't sure if he was scheduled to work that night.

"Hey, Jared! What's up?" *Do I sound casual enough?* I didn't want to overreact and run to the hospital if nothing was wrong.

"I'm getting ready for work, why?"

Okay, there it is. He asked me why, and I have to tell him the truth. "I'm not sure, but I think I'm having a heart attack."

"I'll be right there!" Jared hung up and was at my door within minutes.

This time it was Jared racing me to the hospital. As soon as we told the greeter that we suspected I was having a heart attack, they took me right in. My blood pressure was unusually high. I thought I heard the nurse say that the top number was over 200. She asked if I had forgotten to take my medication. I've never had high blood pressure. No, I don't take medication. It's always been 120 over 80.

The blood work came back and indicated that I wasn't having a heart attack as my enzyme levels were not high, and the EKG looked fine. Relief! I had overreacted and erred on the side of caution. I sheepishly asked the attendants if they thought I had done the right thing by coming to the hospital, even though it turned out that I wasn't having a heart attack.

"Better safe than sorry," they said. I had done the right thing.

I had read that sometimes hospital emergency room physicians don't catch a woman having a heart attack because the symptoms are so different from men's. So Jared and I had decided on the way to the hospital that I wouldn't leave until I saw a cardiologist. He was going to advocate for me in case I caved and wanted to go back home, or if hospital personnel said that I didn't have to stay. But it was a battle we didn't have to fight, because the doctor on duty admitted me so the tests could be run again in a few hours. He also said that I needed to see a cardiologist in the morning. Confident that all was well, I sent Jared off to work and said I would call him in the morning after I saw the cardiologist.

Four hours later, the news changed when blood tests and an EKG were run again in the middle of the night. I *had* experienced a heart attack, or at the very least, what doctors called a heart episode. Typical of a woman having a heart attack, my enzyme level changes showed up later than a man's would have. I really had done the right thing by coming to the hospital with my first symptoms.

A cardiologist came to see me Saturday morning, and I appreciated that he talked to me like a person and not an old lady who had "suffered a heart attack." We made the decision to do a catheterization and inject dye into my heart to see what was happening.

I was given a conscious sedation, which relaxed me so I

wouldn't move during the procedure but still enabled me to be awake enough to watch. The dye could barely get through one of the three main arteries, which indicated that there was a blockage, so we made a decision to put in a stent. It was now Saturday afternoon, and the cardiologist suggested sending me by ambulance to the Meijer Heart Center in town where the procedure could be done immediately. It was a decision that changed my life.

I was not even allowed to walk to the ambulance myself, but had to be wheeled in a bed. The EMT strapped me in so I wouldn't fall off in case the ride was bumpy. As I was rolled into the ambulance, I tried to joke with the EMT to make myself feel more at ease. I made the comment that I had never ridden in an ambulance before. I was used to running a classroom and being in control of my surroundings, but at this point I had no control over anything. I was starting to feel elderly, and I didn't like it at all.

Once I was in the ambulance, I suddenly felt the overwhelming premonition return – that sense of impending disaster – and I could no longer talk. In fact, it felt as if I would choke if I tried. My heart started beating faster, and I could feel my blood pressure rising. My head started hurting. *What was this all about?* The driver shut the back doors of the ambulance, and the other EMT sat down next to me. I could hardly take a breath. I couldn't be having a heart attack because the symptoms weren't the same, and the physicians had thinned my blood. *At least if something is going wrong, I am in the right place.*

All at once, I got a sense of being lifted out of my body and becoming larger so that my energy didn't fit in my body any more. It was an odd sensation that I had never had before. I looked wildly around the ambulance, trying to get my bearings. It didn't help. Something bigger than me was happening. I decided to close my eyes, breathe, and go into a meditative state.

Suddenly, I sensed that Connor was lying on top of me, and he was bleeding. I felt him. It was Connor, and he was hurt. *No, it couldn't be.* I remembered that Kameron had ridden in an ambulance several years before when he had broken his femur. *Maybe that was the image I was remembering? No, this was Connor lying on my chest.* My mind could not make sense of it. *What did it mean? Was I still loopy from the conscious sedation?* I couldn't even take a deep breath. My whole body became heavy and thick. I was acutely aware of every part of myself.

Instinctively, I wrapped my arms around Connor and held him. When the attendant saw me put my arms across my chest, he quickly asked if I was okay. Was I in pain? "No, I'm just giving myself a hug," I replied softly without opening my eyes. How could I explain it to him, when I was struggling to make sense of this myself? I rode this way to the hospital, cradling Connor. I didn't cry and I didn't feel despair because I was totally engulfed by a heavy love. I willed myself to talk to him and tell him that everything was okay. Cradling our sweet boy, I told him over and over how much I loved him.

Connor always loved intertwining hugs. It was something we had done since he was a baby. We would wrap ourselves around each other – legs, arms, heads, and hearts. We spent long moments in such embraces. Connor always said that we were "one" when we hugged like this. Then, as we released our physical embrace, we would look at each other and stay connected, even though we weren't physically touching anymore. Once, after such a hug, he ran downstairs to play, and a few minutes later he hollered up the stairs, "Hey Nana! We're still one!" He said he loved that feeling and felt he was a better person because he was completely connected to me.

We were united in this way once more, during our ambulance rides, even though I couldn't make sense of my experience at the time. I gave myself over to being with Connor. God allowed me to hold Connor in one last, intertwining hug. My ambulance ride was two days before Connor died.

It was as if time was suspended, or as if time didn't exist. I feel certain that God gave Connor the same gift on his ride in the ambulance on Monday night, and it is my sense that Connor also knew I was holding him and that he heard me say over and over how much I loved him. I can't begin to understand how Connor could have felt me holding him. I just know that he did.

Of all the miracles I experienced, this is the one that touched me the most. It was the most incredible gift God could have given me. It may be difficult for others to imagine how difficult it was to let Connor go, but my heart was soothed, knowing that he wasn't alone on his ride to the hospital. It was so comforting to know that, after Connor turned to look at Dani and spoke his last word, "Momma," he felt me take him in my arms, gently holding him for all of us who loved him here on earth. It was an honor to give him back to God. We were one. We always will be.

I choose to think of my heart episode as another gift from God. My heart broke ahead of time so that I could bear the pain in smaller pieces, not in one fell swoop. On Monday, exactly one week prior to the day that Jamarion stabbed Connor, my heart had begun to break. Several days later, on that Friday night, it broke some more. Physically, my heart was repaired two days before Connor died. If the stent had not been put in, I may very likely have suffered a massive heart attack the night Connor was attacked.

Thank you, God. You are a merciful God.

Heartprints

"Given the scale of life in the cosmos, one human life is no more than a tiny blip. Each one of us is a just visitor to this planet, a guest, who will only stay for a limited time. What greater folly could there be than to spend this short time alone, unhappy or in conflict with our companions? Far better, surely, to use our short time here in living a meaningful life, enriched by our sense of connection with others and being of service to them." – Dalai Lama XIV

Every moment of my life has led me to this place in my heart: to be a Nana. Even when he was a little boy, Connor always started our conversations with "Hey Nana!" Whenever I heard those words, I knew something delightful would follow. He amazed me because, from the time he was very young, he was a big thinker and asked many bigger-than-little-boy questions.

Connor used this phrase so much that when his little brother, Riley, began talking, he thought my name was "Hey Nana!" Riley would say, "I love you, Hey Nana." Connor continued to use this phrase, and years later, when Morgan began to talk, he also called me "Hey Nana!" He would ask his parents if he could go to Hey Nana's house.

I have wondered if Connor somehow knew that he was going to die. In thinking of our Hey Nana conversations in the months before his death, I have remembered little things that he shared which were not quite in the same realm as his previous thoughts.

Since Connor and Kamcron attended Excel, I was their music teacher as well – what a great thing! I got to sing and play with my grandsons in their classes. They would visit me before school, and most days after school they came in for a snack, started their homework, or played games while waiting for Jared or Dani to take them home. On the last day of school each year, the boys and I would go out for lunch and then to a kids' movie to start our summer vacation right away.

After the last day of school in June 2014, we were on our way to eat lunch before going to see the movie *Maleficent*. Connor started his query from the back seat. "Hey Nana! I know we've talked about this before, but what do you really think happens when we die?" I wasn't sure what he was asking me specifically this time, so I asked him to tell me more. He said he wanted to know what I thought happened when you died and left your body, and what did I believe happened after that.

Hmmm...pretty big question. I started out by saying that I had come to believe that death was a creative opportunity to begin anew. I waited. Connor was thinking about that.

Then he laughed from the back seat, and I heard him slap his leg. "I really like that. That's a perfect way to think of death – I think I'll believe it, too. A creative opportunity to begin anew."

I checked my rearview mirror and saw him smiling and looking out the window. He had settled the information comfortably into himself. End of conversation. Enough said. He would ask more another day, I knew.

A few days later another question came. "Hey Nana! When you die will you promise to come back and see me?"

Connor and I had had this conversation before as well. When my dad made his transition a few years ago he would come back to visit me, and I would hear his voice in my head. Daddy was particularly worried about me because my husband and I had divorced. I was a single mom with two boys, and he wanted to make sure I was okay.

Connor loved my stories of how my dad would come back and talk to me. I didn't see Daddy; he would just start talking to me. I could actually hear his voice in my head. Whenever Connor and I talked about the fact that I would die someday (a subject he would bring up, not me), he always wanted to hear a story about my dad talking to me. Each time I shared such a story I would say that, no matter what, I would always be in Connor's heart. In response to his question on this day as well, I told him that when I died, he would only need to think of me and I would be there, loving him in his heart. This is my truth. I imagine that I am in the hearts of those I love, and their hearts are my home. I've always believed that this is how we are all connected to each other constantly.

After I answered his question, Connor became quiet. I waited, knowing that he needed time to think. Finally, he said very softly, "And Nana, if I die first, I promise I will come back to see you." I was stunned. This had never come up before.

I remember wondering why he had added that statement. He didn't appear anything but calm and gentle, as always. He didn't seem to be fretting or worried about it, although he was quieter than usual, contemplative.

Throughout our last summer, whenever I spent time with the boys, Connor lingered near me. He was a very active little boy, so this was unusual. Instead of playing downstairs in the toy room with his brothers, he would sit with me on the couch. Sometimes he just sat close, and other times he would sit on my lap and stay there for a long, long time. He spoke quietly and gently about things he loved and how beautiful the world was. He was full of wonder and seemed to be seeing things for the first time. Or maybe he was loving them for the last time.

Looking back, I thought that this was a new and maturing Connor. He was nine years old now, and I assumed that he was coming into a new understanding about his place in the world. I loved this new little boy and his astute observations. At every stage of my children's and grandchildren's lives, I would say how much I loved them and how perfect they were. I wanted them to stay just like that forever. Then they would grow some more, and I would fall in love with them again and want them to stay just like that. Loving a child is a beautiful cycle.

Once that summer, Connor and I were sitting together and looking out at the trees, and he commented on the many different shades of green on one tree. He said the tree looked like all the different people in the world. He loved to watch the breeze moving the leaves and mentioned how it seemed that they became one when the wind blew. I realize now how profound his observations were.

Another time, Connor sat next to me on the couch while I was reading. Even though his brothers were downstairs playing, he was reading his *Captain Underpants* book. He kept moving closer and closer until our sides were touching. He looked up and said, "I love how good it feels to be one with you, Nana."

What if we could all realize that, in every moment of every day, we could all be one. Would the world totally change? It may be the best definition of love: we are all connected. We are all one.

It's interesting that whenever someone dies, you tend to remember the last thing you did together, or your last conversation. The last time Connor and I were together was simple. I had stopped by to pick up something at their house and was waiting in my car in the driveway for Dani to bring it to me. Connor had been playing with his friends and came running over to see me. I had my arm resting on my open window, and he put his cheek on my hand and held it there. Then he looked up, smiled at me, and said, "Hey Nana! You should write a book!"

Wow! Where did that come from? I asked him why on earth he would say something like that. His next words are crystal clear. He said, "Because you know so much, Nana. You could really teach lots of people if you write what you know in a book."

"What do I know that would be worthy of a book?" I asked.

His reply was, "You have so many stories about love, Nana. That's the most important thing you know: love. And you tell those stories so well."

We kissed and did a car-window hug, but he wasn't satisfied with that. He asked me to open my door so that we could have one of our intertwining hugs. I'm so thankful now that we had that moment. I slid my car seat back so that he could sit on my lap as we curled ourselves together. Connor said he loved being one with me, just like always. It was my last, sweet, earthly gift from him. We said our usual "I love you forever," and off he ran, back to his friends.

As I watched him run away, I smiled and thought about how much I loved this little boy. Connor turned, and when he noticed I was watching him he yelled, "We're still one! I know you were thinking about me!" He was full of surprises, and I loved seeing life through his eyes. He turned back yet again, smiled, and gave me a final wave.

He was so dear. Everyone should know a little boy like Connor. He could change people with his love, his smile, his words, his innocence, his joy.

The most beautiful gifts we have received have been stories about Connor that were new to us. So many people have approached us and shared their touching memories of Connor. They may begin with, "I remember one time...," and as soon as I hear those words I imagine myself holding Connor in one of our hugs. I listen to the whole story as I hold him and smile.

It is a curious thing that our brain allows us to transport back into a memory in an instant. Maybe it's because Connor and I were so close that my body is able to remember Connor's smell, the feel of his arms and legs wrapped around me, and his energy becoming one with me. What a gift of comfort God has given me, to always be able to feel that connection with Connor any time I choose.

One story clearly demonstrated Connor's fearlessness and his ability to talk to anyone joyously about love. A neighbor who was a youth pastor at a church told us about a time that he was inside his home. Through his open window, he overheard a gathering of teenagers talk about how they would mistreat their girlfriends and wives when they got older. He was saddened to hear them say how they would "keep them in line with put-downs and beatings." They laughed about how they would abuse their women, and each teenager boasted an even bigger plan for atrocious behavior.

The minister said a prayer and wondered if God would guide him to walk outside, approach the boys, and talk with them about how to be a loving partner. And in the middle of his prayer, he heard Connor start talking to the boys all of a sudden. Apparently, Connor had been riding his bike past the boys and overheard them talking and laughing. Connor couldn't help but share his thoughts. He told the boys how they had it wrong about how to treat their girlfriends and wives. He said you must cherish your partner in order for them to be the best person they could be. Connor added that you must support them, love them, and do kind things for them every day to show them how grateful you are that they love you, too.

The miracle happened. The boys listened to Connor. They didn't make fun of him, ridicule him, or scoff at his thoughts. They listened. The minister said that it was amazing to realize that even God's little children can teach us about love. After delivering his soliloquy, Connor hopped on his bike and rode off. And even then the boys didn't laugh.

I like to think that a seed was planted in their hearts, a seed of love to come. Connor lives on in our world through that little piece of love, which could one day blossom into grander things. I wonder what I have planted in the world? If one little boy could plant such a powerful seed, have I, in my lifetime, planted such goodness?

How could a child to be so fearless? As a teacher, I must admit that walking into the midst of a group of teenage boys to try to change their thoughts and behavior is a daunting task. Yet Connor, who was always very small for his age (about half the teenagers' size and about five years younger than those boys), had a heart that was so big and so full of love, he didn't hesitate to share it. And they listened. That story fills me with such hope – a hope that anyone can change and go on to make a difference in the world. There is no small thing, especially when it comes in the package of kindness and love.

Connor's absolute sense of selflessness frequently caught me by surprise as well. He often thought of others and their needs before his own. When Connor was about five years old I took him, along with Kameron, on a picnic, and we stopped for an ice cream cone afterwards. Connor always ate his cone slowly to relish every lick, while Kameron and I attacked ours, enjoying big bites of ice cream. On this day, Kameron's cone was almost gone when it slipped out of his hand and splatted all over the ground. All three of our mouths dropped open, and we looked at one another. Before I could react, Connor put his arm around Kameron's shoulder and handed his ice cream cone to his little brother, saying, "And now Kameron, you get to try my flavor of ice cream!" The boys ended up sharing Connor's cone while I struggled to keep from crying over Connor's beautiful act of love. It was his nature that brought out the best in me, and still, to this day, inspires me to be a better person.

I loved Connor's gentleness. One time, after he said something mean to his best friend, he cried and cried because he had hurt his friend with his words. Connor was eight years old. How tender hearted he was at such a young age.

A year later, his teacher came to find me because Connor wouldn't stop crying. He was sobbing uncontrollably outside his classroom. I guided him into my music room down the hall and wrapped myself around him. "Did someone hurt you?" I asked as I rocked him and let him cry. Connor sobbed that some of his friends had ignored him on the playground and wouldn't play with him. He said that he now knew what his friend felt like when he had said something mean a year earlier. He was crying because, despite being hurt, he was grateful that his friends had reminded him what rejection felt like.

He kept crying, and I asked him why he could not stop. He answered, "Because I am going to get suspended for crying," and he began wailing again. His teacher had said that he would need to go to the principal's office when he stopped crying, and he knew that when you were sent to the principal's office, you could get suspended.

"No, no, no, Sweetie," I said, "your teacher wants you to see the principal so he can talk with all the boys who were mean to you and help them understand that what they did was wrong."

We both laughed until we cried all over again. This moment was so precious because it revealed to me the purity of [illegible]'s soul. It was one more occasion that I can reflect upon to remind me that we are always one.

A Chance to Heal

What a beautiful name: Jamarion (Jeh-mar-ee-oń). When I say his name, I see his mother holding her beautiful boy for the first time, delighting in her swaddled child, her heart full of love. She names him Jamarion.

I have never met this child who has irrevocably changed our lives. I have seen him, I have felt his energy in the courtroom, and I have looked into his eyes as he turned from the defense table to peer at us. I have read and heard news accounts of his life.

During Jamarion's trial, we heard the recording of the 911 call that he made after he stabbed Connor. Jamarion said he had killed Connor because he was tired of living and wanted to die himself. His voice sounded flat and devoid of emotion as he rattled off facts: the spelling of his name, his location, and how he had stabbed a boy he didn't know. The call lasted over ten minutes, and the only time Jamarion raised his voice was when he felt that the dispatcher wasn't sending the police quickly enough. After the call ended, he knelt in the middle of the street with his hands raised, waiting for the police to arrive, expecting that they would kill him.

The police did not kill Jamarion as he had hoped. Instead, he was taken into custody and driven to a different Grand Rapids hospital than where Connor had been taken. Jamarion claimed to have taken a handful of pills from the medicine cabinet at home, so the police needed to make sure he was examined. His mother, Anita, met him at the hospital, and she was allowed to visit her son with a police officer in the room. Jamarion was hooked up to a machine that monitored his breathing, heart rate, and blood pressure. The officer later testified that, as Anita told Jamarion that Connor had died, there was no change on the monitor. Chilling. Anita told him that he probably wouldn't be allowed to come home again until he was a grown man, and still there was no change on the monitor. After his mother left the room, a single tear rolled down Jamarion's face.

When it was determined that Jamarion was stable enough to talk, a detective recorded his confession. Jamarion lay handcuffed to the hospital bed as the officer read him his rights. He told the officer how he had hidden the knife in his hoodie and intentionally lured Connor, Kameron, and their friend to the playground. On his way to Jared and Dani's house, he had walked past children whom he knew because he didn't want to kill a family member or friend. He even stopped to have a conversation with a neighbor about mowing his yard, all the while contemplating whom he would kill.

This recorded confession from the hospital, along with the

911 recording, provided the judicial system with the facts they needed to charge twelve-year-old Jamarion with open murder. An open murder charge simply means that a murder has been committed; whether or not the crime was premeditated is determined in court. First-degree murder is defined as any intentional murder that is willful and premeditated with malice aforethought. Second-degree murder is also intentional murder with malice aforethought, but it is not premeditated or planned in advance. Additionally, because Connor's murder had been so heinous and seemingly premeditated, some of Jamarion's juvenile rights were waived, and he became the youngest person in Kent County to be charged as an adult. The case became national news: a child had killed another child.

In the year that Jamarion awaited trial, he was held in a juvenile detention facility. A psychiatrist saw him once a month to prescribe medications, and a counselor checked in for a few minutes each day to check on his condition. Jamarion spent much of the time confined to his room because, as the smallest and youngest offender in the detention facility, he was bullied and assaulted. It was reported at trial that Jamarion had tried to kill himself on at least three occasions while in detention.

During Jamarion's time at this facility, he was evaluated by two court-appointed psychiatrists. He revealed to them that he had experienced severe abuse during the course of his lifetime. He also said that, in the year prior to killing Connor, he had tried to cut himself so that he would die, but he couldn't stand the pain. And yet, he was able to inflict such tremendous pain on our sweet Connor.

At the trial, one of the psychiatrists said that Jamarion had told his social worker a year earlier about the abuse he had experienced at home. According to court records, he had been whipped with an electrical cord, and the social worker had taken pictures of his injuries. By law, the social worker was supposed to have reported the abuse to police and remove Jamarion from his home, but she failed to follow protocol. Instead, she made arrangements for him to move permanently to New York with his father and then closed his case file. It was reported at trial that Jamarion had been abused by both his father and grandmother while he lived in New York. After living there for a year, he was sent back to Michigan. Within two months of his return, he stabbed Connor.

The case came to trial in August of 2015. We listened to hours of forensic evidence and witness testimony, which allowed us to fill in the pieces of that horrible day. We found out these details as part of the general courtroom audience, not ahead of time. The jury alone was shown photographs of the scars on Jamarion's legs, arms and back from the time he was abused.

The jury was also shown pictures of Connor, postmortem. We found out that Jamarion had stabbed Connor in his back six times, once so deeply that the knife became stuck in a rib bone. Kameron later said he remembered that stab, because Jamarion had appeared visibly angry when the knife became stuck. This was most likely the wound that severed Connor's lung from his heart and caused his death. A second stab wound to his lung would also have been fatal.

It was also revealed that there had been only minor

traces of antidepressants in Jamarion's system that day. This indicated that, if he *had* taken a handful of pills, it very likely wasn't on the day he killed Connor. When this information was presented, I shivered. Earlier, when I had heard of Jamarion's detached response to Connor's death while he was in the hospital, I had assumed it was because he had overdosed on medications, but this was proof that Jamarion was living so unconsciously that he simply did not care if Connor died.

It was a shock to find out in court that Connor and Jamarion were connected by more than this tragedy. When Anita began her testimony, the defense attorney asked her to provide Jamarion's birthdate. March 14th. Connor's birthday. Stunned, I began to weep, trying to stay quiet so as not to disrupt the trial. We hadn't known this in advance. It seemed so unfair. We couldn't even have Connor's birthday to ourselves – we would always have to share it with Jamarion. It had been my hope that we could celebrate Connor's life every March 14th without the taint of this tragedy, but it was not to be. There would be no escape for us, not even for one day a year.

The trial lasted only two days. The defense attorney's strategy was to prove that Jamarion was mentally ill, due to past abuse. If the jury agreed with the defense, the judge would have the option to commit Jamarion to a mental institution to serve his sentence, rather than to a juvenile facility. It was time for the jury to decide themselves.

During deliberations the jury asked for several things. One thing they asked for was a clarification on the definition of first-degree murder with regard to a defense of mental illness.

They also asked to hear the recording of the 911 call again. We believed that the latter request was because Jamarion's psychiatrist had testified that he'd only meant to poke Connor with the knife, not to kill him. But in the 911 call Jamarion clearly had said, "Hurry and come get me. I just killed someone."

After receiving this information, the jury deliberated for a short time and signaled that they had reached a verdict. They found Jamarion guilty of first-degree murder. The local television stations interrupted regular programming to announce the verdict. It was big news in our city. In Grand Rapids, Michigan, children didn't kill other children. Until now.

Michigan law precludes judges from imposing a life sentence on a child under the age of eighteen who commits a murder, so the district attorney asked for what is known as a blended sentence. This means that the judge has the option to hold Jamarion in a juvenile facility until he is 18 to 21 years old, with the discretion to transfer him to an adult prison for the remainder of his sentence if he is still considered a threat to society. In this way, the judicial system can hold a child responsible for his crime with the understanding that a child who commits murder can't really comprehend the full effect of his actions. Within these sentencing guidelines, there would be hope for Jamarion's rehabilitation.

I awaited the sentencing hearing with prayers from my heart. *I want his life to change. I want him to experience love. I want people to surround him with positive attitudes and praise. He must now live for himself and for Connor. Please,*

God, make it so.

The day before the hearing, court officials were notified of an opening in a juvenile rehabilitation program called the Muskegon River Youth Home. This facility accepts only a few children at a time, and openings are rare. Jamarion's newly appointed advocate spoke to the judge and filled out intake papers so that Jamarion would be accepted to fill the vacancy.

At the encouragement of his mentor, Jamarion read an apology to our family at the sentencing. This man, who runs the prison ministry program at a local church, had pledged to visit Jamarion at the youth facility and counsel him. God could provide no greater gift for Jamarion than to have a strong, positive role model who could lead him into adulthood.

The judge's decision was a blended sentence as the prosecution had suggested. Our family had never discussed our individual hopes for Jamarion's sentence. Nothing could bring Connor back. While Jamarion's fate had never been in our hands, I hoped that the judge's sentence would provide a safe, caring environment for him that would help him heal so that he would have a chance to make a positive contribution to society. I felt strongly that it was important for him to experience the same love that Connor knew in his short life.

I researched the Muskegon River Youth Home online, and from what I read it appeared that Jamarion would live in a homelike environment with boys who were twelve to eighteen years old. The boys are immersed in a positive, caring environment with highly qualified counselors. The residents study together to fulfill academic requirements, with the goal of earning a high school diploma. Jamarion would not only participate in group therapy, but would also meet one-on-one every day with a therapist who specialized in helping children with similar challenges.

For almost two years after Connor was killed, our lives were consumed with the cold and brutal realities of his tragic death and the court proceedings surrounding it. With each new piece of information, we grieved for our Connor, who had befriended this child-turned-monster on one fate-filled day. I had always felt that it had been my life's work to teach, guide, and help thousands of children develop character and become strong productive citizens in our universe, but this nightmare seemed to call everything into question.

At the time of Connor's death, the question that rose so easily from my human nature was "Why? Why did this have to happen to my family, to me? Was this a punishment? Did I deserve this? How could I have done something so horrible for this to be my just reward?"

And then I heard God's clear answer: "If not you, then whom shall I send?"

I was stunned by the thought, but my heart responded, and I began to weep. A complete understanding seemed to settle within me, and I was ready to change my thinking. Memories of times in my life in which I had experienced joy and sorrow, love and fear, compassion and separation began flooding my being. I reminded myself that, every day upon awakening, I ask God to use me for the highest good of his universe. If I lived within this prayer, then I had to believe that God had indeed prepared me for this very moment. My decision seemed simple. Would I choose to live in anger, fear, separation, and hate? Or would I choose compassion, oneness, and love? The answer had to be one or the other, and my conviction needed to be complete.

My purpose changed on this day. I chose to carry God's message of love and compassion to everyone in my life, no matter who they were or what they had done. I was deeply moved and profoundly grateful.

My philosophy as an educator is that teaching involves much more than carrying out a curriculum. As a teacher, I always remind myself to show compassion, love, and forgiveness to students in order to help them grow. If I withhold these qualities, I am sending the message that the child and his actions are not worthy of grace. But I now realize that when people are punished and judged for poor decisions, impulsiveness, or carelessness, they continue to be ensnared in this life. When they are shown compassion and understanding, they develop trust and are able to thrive.

Over my years of teaching, I have taught children of murderers, thieves, abusers, and prostitutes. I have spoken with these parents during parent-teacher conferences and have heard their stories of incredible hardship and challenge. Their children come to school in desperate need of love, attention, and forgiveness. To have any chance for a normal life, parents and children alike need others who will accept them and believe that they can grow to be more than a product of their DNA and environment.

Although the trial had been heart-wrenching for our family, it helped me understand many things about Jamarion's life. Media accounts and court testimony revealed that he had experienced incredible pain and anger. This provided insight into what formed his mental state at the time that he killed Connor. I also learned many things about his family.

Perhaps because of my life experiences, when I saw Anita in the courtroom, I did not see a woman who deserved to be hated or feared. I instead saw a mother who needed compassion. Anita and I would speak briefly during court proceedings, and we have chosen to develop our relationship since the trial. We have discovered that we have much in common. We both came from families in which there were patterns of generational abuse, mental illness, and addiction. Anita and I both want our children to have joyful, healthy lives. Though our past experiences have shaped our adult lives, we have struggled to break the cycle of these maladies so that our children would not suffer as we did.

It is not an easy process. Eradicating these destructive cycles can take generations. Positive, conscious living is necessary in order to create for our own children an environment that is totally different than the one in which we grew up. We are not victims of our DNA, according to scientists in the field of epigenetics. Research has shown that positive interactions and habits can affect gene expression. In other words, children who are raised in an environment of abuse, mental illness, and addiction experience changes in their DNA, which is passed on to the next generation unless positive, conscious living intervenes to change those DNA structures.

As a child, I was angry most of the time when I was around my father. His unpredictability, mood swings, and abuse created an emotionally charged atmosphere in our home. While in public, I learned to pretend that everything was okay, but I was a powder keg ready to explode when he was around. No one knew about the abuse, because I was so good at keeping his secrets. Generational abuse moves surreptitiously to the next generation in this way: the cycle continues because of cover-ups, untruths, and the refusal to see and admit the ugliness and pain of the abuse.

I have spent many years repairing my body, mind, and spirit, in part through counseling and meditating. Researching generational abuse has revealed so much about my past, yet has given me hope for the future. I intentionally surround myself with healthy relationships. Before I considered having children of my own, I needed to be confident that I would not become an abuser myself. I consider myself the first generation to break my family's cycle, and it is my fervent hope that my sons will continue their journey toward healthy living so that our future generations may live free from destructive behavior. I have the same hope for Jamarion's family.

Today, I am able to live in the moment when life is going well, but it is much harder when I face extreme stress or when I am around people who are angry and acting out. When this happens, it is possible to slip back into childhood habits, as my brain was hardwired as a young child to be emotionally reactive around reactive people. This is one symptom of my abuse that I must continue to work on.

Anita has shared that she has begun to find ways to break the cycle through counseling sessions and parenting and other court-mandated classes. While she knew from a young age that she did not want to continue the cycle, she was not able to break free herself and make the personal changes that were necessary to live a different life. Together, Anita and I have eleven children, all of whom have the potential to shift pain and addiction into our next generation. How do we, as human beings, help each other repair generations of damage? Can love really be the answer?

From the time Jamarion was two, Anita has lived with a man who has shared the responsibility of raising Jamarion. He recently pled guilty to charges of child abuse and admitted to whipping Jamarion with the electrical cord. According to Anita, it was the only time that she was aware of abuse. She says that, while her partner was strict with Jamarion, he did not regularly beat him, as was reported in the media and by the psychiatrist at trial. Whether this is the truth, denial, or the secret-keeping that perpetrates generational abuse, we both agree that Jamarion's perception of her partner's strict nature could have spawned his feelings of extreme anger, isolation, hurt, and despair. I believe that this was one contributing factor to the emotional break with reality that led Jamarion to kill Connor.

While in custody, Jamarion has received psychiatric treatment in order to stabilize his emotional and mental state. Mood stabilizers, antidepressants, and psychotropic drugs are included in his regimen and are indicative of a chemical imbalance associated with mental illness, which could have been inherited through generational genetic structures. Likely, it is a second contributor to Jamarion's emotional break.

I believe that addiction was the third factor that led to

Connor's death. When abuse and mental illness exist within a family, addiction becomes a way of self-medicating to ease pain. In listening to court testimony and through conversations with Anita, I learned that every adult in Jamarion's life had come from a background of addiction. When under the influence of drugs, alcohol, or other outlets of addiction, pain is temporarily assuaged, but self-control is inhibited. Negative emotions such as anger can emerge, and the user is more likely to inflict abuse on others. While sober, the abuser may be unlikely to lose control, but under the hold of addiction, the cycle repeats again and again. This was the third strike for the baby named Jamarion.

Jamarion is now getting the help he needs. The judge will review his progress every six months until he turns eighteen. At that time, if the judge determines that Jamarion has been rehabilitated, he will be released. If not, he may be transferred to an adult prison. It depends on Jamarion. For the first time in his life, he has control over his own destiny.

Renewal

"Say not, 'I have found the truth,' but rather, 'I have found a truth.'" – Kahlil Gibran

The aftermath of Connor's death has been full of profound experiences, and I know the truths that I have witnessed do not align with everyone's beliefs. But they have been my experiences, and I know them to be my truth. I have practiced living in the moment and staying open to all possibilities, because at any time a miracle could present itself that changes my understanding about life.

I have learned that when I live in fear, I am not living my best life. For almost a year after Connor's death, I wept uncontrollably every day. Many times I could hardly make it through a day of teaching. I didn't want to cry in front of others, so I would leave school quickly to rush home to what became my ritual of grieving by myself on the couch. Some days, I began sobbing even before I made it to the car. But there came a point at which I had to acknowledge that my grief was all about me, and it was coming from a place a fear. Although this tremendous sorrow was absolutely a necessary part of my healing, eventually I realized that I was grieving for my loss and not for Connor. He was doing just fine with God.

The universe presented me with a choice. It was simple, really. I had to decide if I was going to continue to live in fear and sadness or to celebrate because Connor had been such an integral part of my life, if only for a brief time.

Living with this gaping grief was taking a toll on my body. My cortisol levels were out of control. Cortisol is the fight or flight hormone that is released by the adrenal gland during times of stress. It helps our body produce more sugar energy and suppresses our immune system so that we can survive trauma. However, as I continued to grieve Connor's death, my body, under constant stress, released too much cortisol, which increased my blood pressure, blood sugars, and body weight. I gained 27 pounds in about 35 weeks. I was going to die if I didn't change.

Throughout the year I saw my family doctor and cardiologist regularly. While my body was falling apart, they acknowledged that I needed time to grieve. I am touched that they both had the compassion and understanding to help me move through the majority of my grieving in that year. They prescribed medicines that would keep my heart and body alive until I was ready to live. I didn't like using pharmaceuticals this way, but they were a miracle that I needed.

After almost a year, I began to reawaken to the world around me. I had always meditated and prayed every day, but I began using guided meditations specifically selected to help me awaken to life again. I listened to them in the morning and again at night as I fell asleep. I began cooking healthy foods again instead of eating out of bags and boxes or eating frozen foods that were convenient to prepare, but highly processed. I am grateful for the companies that manufacture those foods, because they kept me alive for the year I wept on the couch.

During that year, it had become my habit to clip up my waist-length hair because I could hardly get out of bed in the mornings, let alone spend time styling my hair. I found a wonderful hair stylist, the owner of Salon Nouveau, who personally makes wigs for children who lose their own hair due to illness. She also specializes in styling curly hair, which I have. I now sport a delightful, low-maintenance hairstyle that makes me smile every morning when I wake up, and a child has a wonderful curly wig that hopefully brings a smile to her face in the morning, too.

In the summer of 2015, I drove to the Tennessee Fitness Spa, where I lived for three weeks surrounded by nature, healthy people, and a wonderful fitness program that allowed me to work at my own level. I began the arduous task of finding myself physically. I took to the spa's indoor swimming pool, as I had always been a water baby, rejuvenated by water. Spa employees allowed me to be in the pool as long as I wanted every day. After a couple of hours of water classes each day, I had the pool to myself to float and play to my heart's content. I relaxed in the sun for an hour each day and attended meditation sessions in the afternoon. Nature, the water, and the sun gently woke me up.

The head chef at the spa made sure that we ate balanced,

healthy meals – no sugar, no salt at all. She allowed me to tap into her wealth of knowledge about healthy cooking and gave me advice about bringing my cortisol levels back in check. The staff prepared protein shakes and a cleansing drink for me every evening. Immediately, my blood sugar leveled off and I began to lose weight.

The spa was located in a beautiful valley, so I also spent time alone, sitting in the woods, connecting with nature as Connor and I used to do. Connor was on to something, even though he was only a little boy. He realized the truth about everything and everyone being connected through our energy at all times if we opened ourselves to this possibility. This was God's gift to me as well: the understanding that when I am one with everything, I am in a state of love. So I practiced. During prayers and meditation, I breathed in and out, feeling a connection with the air, with the chair or floor on which I sat, with my spiritual, emotional, physical, and mental states. As I floated in the pool, or lay in the sun healing, I was consciously part of my surroundings – baby steps towards healing and coming back into life.

Be still and know that I am God. After I left the spa, I continued practicing this stillness until I could find a spiritual state of unity. Anytime I walked outside after being inside all day, I turned my consciousness towards connecting with the outdoors, allowing the wind to wash over me, inhaling deeply, and noticing trees, grass, flowers. All of nature gently enfolded me. At the end of the summer, I returned to teaching, but now when I walked into my home at the end of a long day, I felt a constant state of love instead of deep grief.

When the universe challenged me to change because of Connor's death, I chose to become more of who I was and to enlarge my presence through love in order to honor Connor's life and to honor God, who had given me so many miracles. The universe needs healthy people to participate in raising the consciousness of the human race for its highest good. My evolution in self-awareness was an act of loving myself. As I grow, the universe expands.

After Connor died, I was surrounded by amazing friends and family. I asked for people to continue to hold us in their hearts and prayers because our hearts were broken, and we couldn't go on without their spiritual, physical, and emotional help. This was a humbling experience because I have always had a hard time asking others for help. But now I had no choice because I had been dropped to my knees and could not stand.

So many times, I felt lost – in my darkest days, I had no hope in my heart that I would make it through this. And then another miracle would come. My friends and family were there. They were God's angels who held me completely in their hearts, every moment of every day, until I could lift up my head, my eyes could see, and I had the strength to stand. They held me until the numbness began to subside and my breath flowed again. My loved ones helped God comfort and gently carry me.

It has always been essential for me to surround myself with healthy people, people who are caring, productive, compassionate, and willing to step up to help when the universe needs them. After Connor died, my circle of friends and family saved me and lifted me. I received so many inspiring cards, notes, phone calls, and text messages. I was blessed with meals, gifts, and prayers throughout the year. Whenever I was having a rough day, I would find a gift or a note from someone who loved me. All of these were reminders that I was to live on toward greater things.

People were so generous that I was brought to tears many times and humbled by their love and generosity. A family friend of Dani's set up a GoFundMe account where hundreds of people from all over the world donated money for funeral expenses and sent messages of love to support Jared and Dani. I had never heard of GoFundMe, but at a time when we were emotionally overwhelmed, it was such a relief not to have to worry about bills. Jared, Dani, and I were touched by how many people responded, and we were comforted when we read the personal messages. In total, over $19,000 was raised through GoFundMe.

Another benefactor gave Jared and Dani money through the Kentwood Police Department a week after our tragedy. The gift was anonymous, and we were grateful.

Jared's employer, Hearthside Foods, set up a matching fund for donations. People who barely made minimum wage gave generously to the fund, and the company matched all the monies raised at their plants. We were humbled by their love.

The owners of Jared and Dani's mobile home park took loving care of them. They set up a fund for people who lived in the neighborhood and waived Jared and Dani's lot rent for the months following the tragedy. Their generosity was simply amazing.

My immediate family has been my rock. My sisters and brother called me frequently so that I could cry and talk and share my grief. They supported me emotionally and helped whenever they could to meet our needs.

My friends and coworkers from Excel continued to support us. Many have shared their favorite pictures and stories of Connor over the years, touching our hearts as we see him in all his glory – being a little boy. I experienced the most inspiring love from staff, leadership, and families. They are a living example of God's love and generosity in action.

When Jared and Dani's car was no longer reliable, an Excel staff member donated one. When their washer and dryer broke, another Excel friend provided a used set. Almost every week, we received generous gifts of food and clothing. Jared and Dani lost their jobs because they were struggling to function, so the staff members of Excel surprised us at Christmastime by providing grocery store gift cards, clothes, and toys for the family. It was an amazing example of a village working together.

Other colleagues continued to lift me up. I teach music using a method known as Education Through Music (ETM). Over the past twenty years I have travelled throughout the United States, learning to teach the whole child through ETM's music and play. Many of my friends in this program, who live across the country, were so very kind, prayerful, and generous. Their love and support prepared me for singing and playing with Excel's children every day, and I began to smile and laugh again.

Our family felt such comfort and love. We were able to put

one foot in front of another as friends met our spiritual, emotional, and physical needs. When people helped us, I realized that the physical world was God's gift to us. When given in love, there is no small thing.

I experienced God's miracles all around me during this time of deep mourning. With simple things: medicine, food, swimming, the sun, gifts, and friends, God put His miracles in my life daily, and all that was required of me was to receive them gratefully.

And yet, our lives were turned upside down. Nothing was the same. We had to learn to live a new normal without Connor. Even though we were surrounded with love and care from friends and family, the emptiness was huge. Never before in my life had I felt so much raw, gaping, and overwhelming emotion. Many times, the distance between my head and my heart was massive, and I was in utter despair.

The day after Connor was killed, I prepared breakfast for his brothers. Our ritual was to join hands at the dining room table, say a prayer, and then eat. I remember feeling numb as I called the boys to the table. We sat down, and then it hit us. We realized that Connor wasn't in his chair, and we couldn't complete our circle of joined hands without him. Morgan looked around with panic in his eyes. He sobbed, "How can we ever eat again? We can't say prayers without Connor!" My grandsons and I broke down sobbing.

Our pain was so great that we couldn't even comfort each other. We sat separately, crying. There was no human comfort to be had at that table. I don't know how long we cried, but there finally came the moment when we had to go on with our lives. Kameron, Riley, and Morgan began to figure out a way in which we could all join hands to say our prayer. I was so devastated that I could only watch them. For the first time in their lives, Nana wasn't able to help. The boys finally came up with a solution. We had to sit in every other seat, then Kameron lay across the table to hold Morgan's hand, and we all stretched to grasp hands and pray. We cried the whole time we were praying. It was hard to give thanks for our first meal without Connor.

Since Connor's death, Morgan has seemed to be the one who was not afraid to face his grief. As a three-year-old, he grieved deeply and then found the right moment to move on and live in a new way. He lived in the moment, in the now. Sometimes, I have found life lessons in unlikely places, and Morgan has shown me how to lovingly remember Connor in our everyday experiences.

I wonder how Morgan will remember his oldest brother, because he was so young when Connor died. However, Morgan will pipe up to remind me that he does remember him. Recently, I took the boys to McDonalds, and as we waited for our order Morgan said, "I miss Connor, and I wish he was still here with us. He would have loved getting some chicken nuggets today." I smiled through my tears and nodded.

This was how we began to heal. We grieved until the moment came to live on. Then, we had to stretch ourselves as we had at the table to find a new way to live without Connor. Finally, we had to repeat it over and over for weeks and months until it felt normal to live this way – a new normal, without Connor. It has been a monumental task.

I am so sad to live on without Connor. I don't know if or when that sorrow will ever leave my heart – it seems such a part of me now. But I am eternally grateful for the opportunity to have experienced the tremendous love, compassion, and kindness that lives in the hearts of so many people and the healing I have received because of it.

Journey Toward Love

What I know for certain is that we need more compassion in this world so that we can become all we are meant to be. Compassion is love in action.

With a renewed self-awareness of who I am in the physical, emotional, mental, and spiritual realms, I find myself to be more observant and content, and less reactive in my everyday life. I am struck by the absolute beauty in everyone and everything around me. I had experienced God's absolute love in the hospital after Connor died, and this experience has allowed my heart to see others differently.

Curiously, I'm often struck by the contrast in how people are treated. After Connor's death, my family and I were so blessed by an outpouring of love and generosity. For me, it was another miracle to receive the best of human nature as people helped, prayed, and showered us with support during this time. That loving energy has helped me heal from a tragedy that I didn't think I could live through. But what about Jamarion and his family? Who held *them* in their hearts and prayers? Who sent them cards, food, and love so that they could heal? Was a GoFundMe account set up to help them through this experience? Why does our human nature allow us to decide that only some people are worthy of love and compassion?

My epiphany has been that I can no longer deceive myself into believing that donating my used clothing, giving to Toys for Tots, and serving in our homeless programs were active acts of compassion. While these gifts were necessary and very much appreciated, they were anonymous, passive acts. What I experienced personally during this tragedy was that engaged, interactive acts of compassion helped me to become more of who I am. I was humbled by the love and altruism of family, friends, and strangers. I grew because of the *people* who surrounded me. With this knowledge, I wonder how I can do more. What will my love in action look like?

Nothing changes if nothing changes, as the saying goes. So I choose to change how I respond to people in need and to make a difference where I feel I can personally demonstrate my love and compassion by developing a personal relationship with others. If society's response to our family's tragedy is simply to put Jamarion away for a number of years and shun his family, then we may be creating a bigger problem by perpetuating unhealthy cycles. So I feel compelled to show Jamarion and his family acts of love and compassion, in hopes of helping them to heal and grow.

After Jamarion stabbed Connor, we found out that Anita lost her job because she worked for the same company as Jared. We heard that some employees threatened to kill her if she returned to work. Of all the places to work in Grand Rapids, how was it that she and Jared had the same employer? I took that as another sign from God, reminding me that we are all the same. Yet Anita was treated so differently.

In the weeks following Connor's death, Jared and Dani heard from neighbors that Anita had been walking around their mobile home park in the evenings, knocking on doors to try to find them. She wanted to say how sorry she was that her son had killed Connor. Dani read an interview that Anita had done with *The Detroit Free Press* in which she indicated that she wanted apologize to us. It was the only interview that she allowed. She seemingly did whatever she could to try to ease our pain, even though she had become a pariah to society. I admired her character and great courage, which fueled my resolve to support her.

One news article identified Anita's neighborhood, so Dani and I set out to find her about three weeks after the tragedy. We drove up and down the street, stopping at houses that had toys in the yard because Dani had read that Jamarion had little sisters. Everywhere we stopped, people expressed their sympathy and regret that Jamarion had killed Connor. We finally found Anita's home.

We knocked on the back door, and when Anita looked out the window, I could see in her eyes that she recognized us. I saw anguish and pain in her face. As she opened the screen door, I introduced Dani and myself. Immediately, we all began to sob and hold each other. Anita called into the house for her partner to join us. He began sobbing with us as we were introduced. Over and over, they told us how sorry they were.

There was no doubt that they were grieving as much as we were.

I had written a card beforehand for Anita. I wrote to her as a mother myself and told her how sorry I was that our families were now united for the rest of our lives by this tragedy. We were devastated that she had lost her job and couldn't stand the thought that she might not be able to feed her children that week, so we included grocery money.

While our time together was comforting, I also felt overwhelming distress. I was still numb. I felt as if I were living in a huge bubble of pain and unreality. Here we were, Dani and I, holding on to Jamarion's parents.

I couldn't even imagine what it felt like to know that your young son had murdered another child. Along with deep anguish, there had to be feelings of shame and guilt. I tried to imagine what it would be like, but it was too overwhelming, I had to back off that emotional precipice. I could not envision myself in Anita's shoes. It was too much for me.

We spoke quietly for a short while. No reporters, no attorneys, no outside interference – just the four of us talking about the tragedy that united us. This moment was another miracle for me. I truly experienced the feeling that we were all one. God was clear about that for me. I could not defy God's love by remaining separate from Jamarion and his family.

I think that if Anita and I had met under normal circumstances, we could have been friends. While I was trying to put myself in her shoes, trying to understand what she must be going through, she said that she was doing the same. She tried to imagine having a son, a grandchild, murdered by another child. She noted that, while she could still talk to Jamarion and hug him and visit him, we did not have that luxury with Connor. She said she couldn't imagine what we must be going through. The feeling was mutual.

Anita realized that the press would report that she had been a bad mother. But she said that she had done the best she could, especially with Jamarion. I asked her if she'd had any idea that Jamarion was capable of or wanted to kill someone. No, she answered honestly, she never saw this coming.

Dani talked briefly about what she had been feeling and how she was interested in joining with Anita to help other parents. She wanted to support mothers of troubled children by finding ways to get help before a tragedy like this happened. Dani recognized that mothers on welfare and Medicaid often found it difficult to find the necessary treatment for a mentally and emotionally ill child.

Our time together was an opportunity that most people on both sides of a tragedy do not receive. Before the media and attorneys told Jamarion's story, I was able to hear Anita say, "I did the best I could. I am so sorry." I believed her and knew this to be her truth. It made my decision to show compassion and love easier than I would have thought possible.

Throughout the next year, during the court hearings and trial, Anita and I continued to connect and speak in the hallway before we entered the courtroom and sat on opposite sides. Sometimes we sat together during breaks, talking quietly. I wanted Anita to know who we were and who Connor had been. Fortunately, I never hated Anita. Even in my darkest moments, I couldn't hate her. I could only feel compassion and love. I thank God for holding me in pure love for those moments in the hospital. He changed my heart so that I would no longer hate, even amidst all my pain and sense of loss.

I wanted to encourage Anita as well, so I told her about one of my favorite thoughts from the movie *Winter's Tale*: "The universe has a love affair with every human being, none more important than the other. There is nothing that is without purpose."

"You matter," I shared. "Everything you have ever done has mattered. Every day we have a chance to start over. Start again today and live as though you matter. You are important to the universe."

I could tell that Anita struggled to believe it. She shook her head and looked down. I wondered what our world would look like if every one of us internalized this philosophy. If this was the message we saw posted on our bathroom mirrors every day, reminding us how important we were to the universe and how much we were loved, could it bring healing to the world? Is it possible for us to love and honor ourselves so much that we don't feel the need to put others down in order to lift ourselves? Is this a philosophy that could grow compassion in every one of us?

Connor was such a beautiful little boy and, had his life not been cut short, I was sure that he would have continued to befriend Jamarion. I shared my thoughts with Anita. Connor was so loving and so loved. I wanted her to know that Dani and Jared were good parents who loved their boys as much as she loved her children.

I promised Anita that I would make sure Jamarion

received help after his sentencing. I shared that I was appalled that he had been sent to his room in solitary confinement during much of his time awaiting trial, and that he had received so little help during that time. Any mother would be anguished to find her son in that situation. While I couldn't condone Jamarion's actions, I knew that he desperately needed help. If he was simply locked up without qualified counseling, he could be even more damaged upon release.

At first it was hard for Jared and Dani to see me sitting with Anita in the courthouse hallway. Other friends shared that they felt I was betraying Connor's memory by befriending Anita. I tried to help them understand my intentions. When I spoke about my feelings of love and compassion for Jamarion and Anita, sometimes I was met with blank stares. I wondered what my friends were thinking behind those stares. There were times that they walked away from our discussion because they were so frustrated that I did not feel my actions were objectionable. People were offended by my behavior. Fortunately, after we talked several times, Jared and Dani understood my intentions.

To try to understand what my friends were feeling, I looked within to remember times in my past in which I could identify with those same emotions. Why had I felt jealous when my friends had other loving relationships? Why had I worried whether they loved someone else more than they loved me? Could love be measured and quantified? Was I betraying Connor if I showed compassion towards Anita? How could I choose to love some people but determine that others were not loveable, or at the very least, unworthy of my compassion? As

I pondered, I felt my body respond. My stomach became knotted and my throat closed up. I recognized the feelings of unworthiness and fear. My emotions of jealousy, anger, and betrayal were all fear-based. I could change my reaction. I could choose love. Just by acknowledging that I had a choice – fear or love – and then choosing love, I could become more of what I wanted to be. My heart was a heart of love, and showing compassion to Jamarion's family was good and right.

Anita had made an accurate prediction about how she would be portrayed by media outlets. After Connor was stabbed to death, people wanted to blame someone, and Anita became the target. Jamarion's confession included accounts of abuse, and records from several years earlier showed that two of Anita's children were permanently removed from her home after they were found to have symptoms of abuse. Two weeks after Jamarion killed Connor, attorneys from the Michigan Child Welfare Services moved to terminate Anita's parental rights, and her three remaining children were put in foster homes. For months, Anita worked to comply with the court's requirements in order to have her parental rights reinstated, and her children were returned in ten months. Additionally, Anita was charged with and eventually convicted of abusing Jamarion, and she served 120 days in jail. The State of Michigan also charged her with welfare fraud for failure to report income, and she was sentenced to repay $14,000 and perform community service.

In light of these facts it would appear that, if anyone deserved to be blamed for Jamarion's pain, it was Anita. When others spoke of her, I could sense their disdain. But every time

I prayed, I was reminded that I could not cast the first stone. Because of my experience throughout this tragedy, I knew for certain that the only way Anita could heal was for her to receive understanding, compassion, and love. I remembered God's words: if not me, then whom would He send?

In spite of all of Anita's shortcomings, I absolutely believed her statement that she did the best she could with the resources she had. It may not have been what I would have done if I had been in her shoes, but it was her best. Her life and her truth were very different than mine. But without a doubt, she was worthy of compassion and love.

In comparing our lives, I feel that there were two important events that helped me overcome my background of abuse, mental illness, and addiction. The first event was when I was in high school. My mother made the decision to send me to live in Ohio with my aunt and uncle for a summer to separate me from my dad. My uncle was a professor at Youngstown University, and he arranged for me to work with the French horn instructor throughout the summer. Every weekday I went to the university with my uncle to practice, take music lessons, and to be exposed to college life. That summer changed everything. I was able to experience a normal life, and I came to the realization that the world had more to offer me than the experiences of abuse, mental illness, and addiction.

Secondly, my parents encouraged me go to college right after high school. Leaving my home environment for several years exposed me to normal outside influences, allowing me to begin to change the seemingly inevitable path that my DNA and family life predicted I would repeat. I developed a completely different sense of self, realizing that I could choose to heal.

While our childhood influences were so similar, Anita did not have the opportunity to see what else the world had to offer, as she had two children at a young age and found herself repeating the cycles from her childhood. The effects of poverty are complicated and widespread, but not insurmountable if even one person believes in you and helps you step out of your circumstances. I think that the reason Anita and I are so different is because our young adult experiences were so dissimilar. But the good news is that it is never too late to become the person you always knew you could be. Anita can change her truth and choose to heal now. Could I be that person who believes in her?

It has been encouraging for me to hear that Anita has experienced one blessing in the aftermath of this tragedy. While she lost job after job in the first few months after Jamarion stabbed Connor, she finally found a position where management knew about her life and yet made the decision to allow her to keep her job as long as she worked hard. On the days after court hearings and proceedings, when she could barely function, her immediate supervisor sought her out so that Anita could share what she was feeling. He arranged for a work release program so that, while serving her jail sentence, she could continue to do her job. Anita had found one person with a fully compassionate heart, and she was immensely grateful. Because one man showed compassion, Anita was able to survive this most difficult time. One person truly can change the world.

In our talks since she has been released from jail, Anita has said that she is learning to find her voice to speak out against abuse. She had experienced abuse as a child, and remembered claiming to herself that she would change the world someday so that others wouldn't suffer as she had. I shared with her that I had vowed the same thing when I was little. Maybe together we can accomplish this. Is it possible that the answer is love?

Anita and I both come from families in which abuse, mental illness, and addiction were rampant. Experiencing these three things changes who you are. Many of us aren't able to overcome the results of addiction and abuse without extensive counseling, education, and hard work. For me, it took leaving my home environment, therapy, and constant spiritual attention to learn to live consciously. I have chosen to be deliberate in every choice to ensure that I am making healthy decisions, working to fully engage in every moment so that my future will be more than my past declared I should be.

My conviction is to hold love in my heart and continue my quest to search inward. I am committed to behold myself through eyes of love, rather than fear. I will ferret out my insecurities, my prejudices, and my feelings of unworthiness that hold me back from being my best self.

I have collided in the universe with a family that was so similar to mine, with devastating results. I am compelled to ask myself: *To what end?* And then I remember Connor. *Oh yes! It is about love!* In his short life on earth, Connor taught me that we must be purposeful with love. Although I cannot change the past, I have the ability to choose my response. I believe that it is our destiny to love each other and that compassion is the vehicle that demonstrates our love. Connor knew this, and he lived it.

I wonder if God sends souls to this earth temporarily to teach us a more authentic way to live. We will never know what impact Connor would have had on the world if he had been given the chance to live a longer life, and in the absence of that knowledge, his life of nine years will be judged as complete. While he walked with us, he imparted the monumental gift of altruistic love.

Today, I am able to think of Connor and smile. I do not know if tomorrow will be as gentle with me, and I accept that it may come with pain and tears. But every day, I am reminded of the imprint that Connor left on the universe as he touched people with his heart of love. When he was suddenly taken from us, so many people were compelled to treat others in a purer fashion because of his gifts of love, forgiveness, and compassion.

As one person grows, the universe expands, and as thousands grow, the universe expands exponentially. I am so honored to know that Connor's life has created such a powerful expansion, and as I am reminded that Connor and I are one, I am sure that he would be pleased, too. On my beloved grandson's behalf, from my heart to yours, I offer Connor's story of love.

Acknowledgements

The experience of writing and producing a book has challenged me to become more than I thought I could be. When Connor told me one day that I should write a book, I had no idea what the process fully entailed. Fortunately, with the help and support of many friends and family, I tell you his story.

First, I would like to thank my friend and editor, Betty Epperly, who had heard that I wanted to write a book about Connor. She offered her expertise one fall day saying, "I will have some time in February to take a look at your book if you'd like." I smile and chuckle to myself as I recall that I thought this meant we would have the book done in February. Almost a year later, we are ready to present our work to readers. I'm not sure that either of us knew what my book would look like all those months ago, but thank you, friend, for walking beside me, pushing from behind, and leading by example so that Connor's story would be our gift to the world. You have been a great joy in my life these past months.

In addition to the written word, I would like to thank artist Laurie Sienkowski for giving my ideas physical beauty. I am grateful for your time and willingness to demonstrate my story with pictures I couldn't even imagine until you put them onto paper.

I am also thankful for my sister, Jan Nunemaker, who walked through this tragedy with me from the first phone call. Your kind spirit, gentle ways, and your unwavering faith in God buffered me so that I could come back to life and live strong once again.

My girls' weekend friends, Education Through Music friends, and Excel Charter Academy family have been my rock on a daily basis, holding my heart in theirs throughout my grieving process. This book is a testament to your love in action. I am especially grateful for Ryan Winter, my friend and dean at Excel, for always making time to let me talk, cry, and grow, and for the many times I just needed to pray with you so I could hold on one more day.

I would also like to thank Ken Kolker from WOOD TV for his kindness throughout the past two years. His diligence as a reporter uncovered mistakes that had been made by Child Protective Services and generated changes in the system so that other children are better protected than Jamarion had been. He also kept us informed of proceedings and updates so that our family felt we could be actively involved in the justice system on Connor's behalf.

My sons, Jared and Keevan, and daughter-in-law, Dani, have given me an incredible opportunity to become a better mother, Nana, and woman with a heart of love I didn't know was possible. I love you all so dearly.

Finally, I am so grateful for my beloved grandson, Connor, who knew before I did that I had a book about love hidden in my heart.

Made in the USA
San Bernardino, CA
14 January 2017